W9-BNJ-983

What people are saying about *By the Time You Read This . . .*

In this, her final message to the world, Cheslie is authentic and raw, bridging the gap between her public persona and the personal challenges she faced. Her words, heartbreaking and beautiful, are a cautionary tale for anyone who has wrestled with self-doubt and struggled to recognize their value. A must-read for all young women finding their place in the world.

——**PAULA SHUGART,** Former President, the
Miss Universe Organization

This book reminds me that hope, like a mother's love, is boundless, and in our darkest moments, we need only be reminded that these are the footprints in the sand that have carried us throughout. In sharing Cheslie's light and love, April encourages readers to give themselves "space and grace," to know that their life is worth living, and that they are not alone in their struggles.

——**DR. SUE VARMA,** Author of *Practical Optimism:*
The Art, Science, and Practice of Exceptional Well-Being

I did not realize I could admire and appreciate Cheslie more. I saw her, I heard her, and I felt her. Every chapter shares insight into her strength and passion for friendship, family, women, social justice, her community, and her identity. Every page radiates with her spirit. Every word has a resounding effect, which captivates us as she pours her entire being into this book. Her story illustrates her purpose, and her legacy lives in every life she has and will continue to touch. Thank you, Cheslie, for being forever selfless.

——**RACHEL LINDSAY,** Attorney and Media Personality

Reading this powerful and provocative manuscript brought both tears and smiles. Knowing the depth of Cheslie's pain while she was abundantly sharing her gifts with Dress for Success Charlotte and so many others, gives me a great appreciation for what her mother, April, has captured. Each and every day Cheslie was with us was a victory. Her victory. Our victory. And her sharing her struggle with mental health will forever be part of her legacy. She has helped us move conversations around mental health from words to activation. In fact, more than forty Dress for Success Charlotte clients are now certified QPR Gatekeepers as a result of our relationship with Cheslie. QPR stands for *Question. Persuade. Refer*. With this innovative, practical, and proven suicide prevention training, our new Gatekeepers are better positioned to save lives and reduce suicidal behaviors. We are honored to continue to move forward her wish to raise awareness, educate our community, and contribute towards a stigma-free society. Well done, Cheslie!

—**KERRY BARR O'CONNOR**, Executive Director,
Dress for Success Charlotte 2005–2023

BY THE TIME YOU READ THIS

THE SPACE BETWEEN CHESLIE'S SMILE AND MENTAL ILLNESS

Her Story in Her Own Words

CHESLIE KRYST AND APRIL SIMPKINS

Forefront
BOOKS

Published by Forefront Books, Nashville, Tennessee.
Distributed by Simon & Schuster.

Library of Congress Control Number: 2024901340

Print ISBN: 978-1-63763-300-7
E-book ISBN: 978-1-63763-301-4

Cover Design by Bruce Gore, Gore Studio, Inc.
Interior Design by Bill Kersey, KerseyGraphics

Printed in the United States of America

*Net proceeds from the sale of this book will be used to support the
Cheslie C. Kryst Foundation, which was founded in Cheslie's honor.*

This book is dedicated to the millions who battle mental illness in the shadows. May it help you come into the light, find your support tribe, and live another day.

To those who've lost someone to their mental health battle: I see you. I feel your pain. You are not alone. Keep pressing forward.

And finally, to the tribe from which we hail: David, Page, Asa, Chandler, Brooklyn, Jet, Raegan, and Rodney. Thank you. We love you.

CONTENTS

PREFACE

Dear Cheslie,

Through tears, I read your manuscript in early 2022, not long after you left this life to move on to the next. I tried to stay open-minded and absorb the words you left behind. I cried for you and with you, poring over the pages, reliving many of the events you shared. I wanted to pause and ask you for more details, to better understand some of your decisions. How deeply the emotions you vividly described resonated with me! More than anything, I wanted to hug you and tell you, "You're not alone, baby girl."

The first time I read your manuscript, I was looking for something. Maybe answers or a revelation. Perhaps a specific moment or event that might shed light on the feelings you wrote about—loneliness, hopelessness, and sadness. I read your words and felt the turmoil, the struggle, the pain. I felt your heartaches, your heartbreaks, and your disappointments. Reading your words and knowing that in the background you were battling persistent depression speaks to how hard you fought for your mental health.

When you were in middle school, I met with your guidance counselor. You had tested so high in your academics that they wanted to send you to a special school for exceptionally gifted students. The guidance counselor praised your drive, your push for perfection, and your extreme intelligence. And then she pointed out the thorns—how children with your level of drive can burn themselves out without realizing it. I recalled instances when your self-imposed level of perfection compelled you to rewrite an entire paper because you had crossed out something, which made the paper look less than perfect. Even into your adulthood, I always marveled at your incredible determination. I used to feel like you were ignoring me when I'd tell you to take some time off, slow down, delegate. (Remember when I tried to convince you to hire a personal assistant? Good times. LOL!)

I want you to know, baby girl, that I read your words and listened—I heard you.

As you instructed me in your final wishes, I'm seeing to it that your book gets published. My hope is that as people read your book— especially the parts where you shared what you were thinking and feeling behind the scenes of your work life and some of your most iconic achievements—they find themselves understanding you and empathizing with you. May people feel compelled to reevaluate where they are in life and seek balance and support for their own mental health.

Thank you, Cheslie, for every day you fought and won your battle with depression. Thank you for every day you focused on being a light in this world. Thank you for making a difference in the lives of so many during your time on this earth. Thank you for the years you spent taking care of your mental health. And thank you for the time you spent with me.

You were wonderfully and beautifully made by God. You lived your best life, and I'm proud of you for that.

You are and will forever be loved, baby girl.

Forever yours,
Mom

PART ONE

Cheslie's Story

INTRODUCTION

E w!" he sniffed. "Did you take a bath?"

One of my seventh-grade bullies was starting up his latest attack in the lunchroom. I wanted so badly for him to like me, to approve of me, that I never made fun of him or said anything harsh in my own defense.

"No—I take showers," I retorted, thinking I was being clever. It didn't matter. My bully started loudly laughing before I could finish my answer, drowning out my response.

Middle school was when the real teasing began for me. It's when I realized I wasn't popular or pretty. It was when I noticed I had a unibrow, which wasn't cool. It's when I first started wearing glasses for my terrible eyesight, caused by years of reading books at night with the lights off. Bedtime always came too soon, and it always seemed that I'd reached the good part in the chapter just when it was time to flip off the light switch. I never did my hair and kept it pulled back in the same bun behind my head, most days without taking it down to redo it or wash it. And I had no sense of style.

My family moved across town in the middle of my torturous seventh-grade year, which meant I'd be at a new school come eighth grade. That was the year I decided I was going to reinvent myself. My sister was in high school by then and loved playing with my waist-length hair. I figured it was time to talk to her about doing it in some pretty styles, flat-ironing it and putting it in intricate braids, like Alicia Keys wore in her music videos. I'd grown tall enough to be able to fit into some of my mom's clothes and, as Mom had recently gotten divorced and was newly back in the single world again, she had some fresh, cute new items that she let me borrow regularly. I made the cheerleading team, earned some cool new friends, and even had my first boyfriend—although we only ever talked to each other at lunchtime and dated for all of two weeks.

My plan continued when I got to high school. I made the cheerleading team again, earning myself invitations to a few parties and hangouts with the cool kids, but on the inside I still felt like the ugly girl with yellow teeth and a unibrow.

I soon added competing in pageants to my I-never-want-to-be-bullied-again plan. My mom had won Mrs. North Carolina US 2002 when I was a kid, and I distinctly remember sitting on the side of the road during a parade, watching her roll by in a white horse-drawn carriage. Her mint-green, two-piece ball gown gracefully draped from her body to the floor as she waved to people gawking at her on the street. I idolized my mom and knew if I could win a pageant, I could be beautiful just like her. I could be heard.

The plan worked. I competed in pageants for years, and even though there were always a few days or periods of time when I didn't feel confident, my self-esteem grew. People asked me time and time again why I competed. Even as the popularity of pageants declined and their place in society was questioned, I could always give a laundry list of answers. Earning scholarship money. Being a part of a sisterhood. Sharpening my interview skills. Unlocking new opportunities to reach people with a platform or message that was important to me. Having an extra layer of motivation to exercise. Although those answers were true for me, I never shared the one reason I started competing in the first place, for fear that in the politically correct, highbrow circles of pageantry, it would sound shallow. At age fourteen, I started competing for validation.

My high school pageant didn't have community service requirements or offer a cash prize or include any responsibilities after I won. I signed up because I needed to be pretty. I wanted some way to measure that I was worthy, whether that was having boys ask for my phone number, growing my hair as long as possible, or winning a pageant title. Thankfully, the pageants I continued to compete in as I grew older had evolved enough to provide additional benefits and truly shaped who I am now, but young Cheslie wanted little more than that moment of looking into an audience seated behind a panel of judges, knowing the crown on my head meant I met their approval.

Unfortunately, the initial reason I craved a win on the pageant stage was also what cast pageantry into limbo in modern society. People thought pageant queens were pretty, but that's all the credit they gave us. Year after year, there were fewer people who cared to watch pageant competitions and more people who claimed that pageants were misogynistic relics that elevated empty-headed women.

In 2019, what place did pageants have in society?

It was an important question for me to answer, especially as a practicing attorney. If I was going to continue to compete as a grown, twenty-eight-year-old woman, there had to be some reason for it beyond wanting to be considered beautiful—which was something I no longer needed from pageantry, as my confidence had increased over the years.

The way I saw it, titleholders were a mix of influencers and activists. In a world where talk of stretch marks, "real bodies," and destroying colorism had gained popularity, women in pageants strutted across stages in their muscular, thin, curvy, bodacious, flat-chested, short, and tall glory, living out the message that many were posting about on their social media platforms. Pageant titleholders spoke before legislatures across the country and at the United Nations, galvanized their communities behind important causes, and used international costume competitions to spread messages like "Stop Asian Hate," "Pray for Myanmar," and "No more hate, violence, rejection, [and] discrimination."

The only people I met who didn't understand and support the evolution pageantry had made over the years were those who hadn't watched a pageant in a decade but had been pulling up old, flubbed onstage questions on YouTube to laugh at with their friends.

Whether people understood or not, I knew the benefit I had to gain from competing. And from winning.

As I stood waiting for the Miss USA competition to start, I soaked in the joy of being minutes away from stepping onto the biggest stage I'd ever been on, after years of my own evolution.

Chapter 1

GOD HAD A PLAN

I t was May 2, 2019, and I was in a hotel room in Rer already starting to clench in my gut.

I'd spent almost two weeks in the crowded room I with Miss Louisiana USA and our piles of luggage. Victoria a personable, gorgeous, and slender blonde woman whom clicked with almost immediately upon meeting her. She was caretaker by nature, and almost every time I talked to her, she offered to connect me with a new clothing sponsor or impart some helpful advice she'd learned or shoot me a compliment just when I needed it. I couldn't imagine rooming with a more pleasant and accommodating person, and even then I was Ready. To. Go.

The Miss USA competition was far more than the television broadcast aired on finals night. It was two long weeks of being on-site to acclimate to the time difference and weather, do promotional photoshoots and sponsor-related appearances, visit local destinations, shoot content for the night of the show, rehearse dance numbers, and take on the preliminary competition. Some of us were also paranoid that the contestant chaperones were relaying messages about our behavior to the head of the Miss Universe Organization (MUO) or keeping a tally of the

er of times we were late to a scheduled event. Of course,
one running the big show assured us this wasn't the case,
who would take that chance? The competition felt like weeks
being on your A game every moment of every day, and I was
rnt out.

Despite my exhaustion, the finals day jitters gave me the
park I needed to roll out of bed that morning. I did my full hair
and makeup routine before hopping into an elevator to head
down to breakfast, ready for the dress rehearsal afterward.

Walking into the restaurant for breakfast and greeting the
other women in the competition didn't help my anxiety one bit.
Even though many pageants had evolved over the years from
calling themselves "beauty pageants" to insisting on using the
word *competition*, the "beauty" part never left. Breakfast was
basically a fashion show with a side of eggs and toast, and the
women I was competing against had turned the stove burner on
high for our last day of competition.

There were two-piece crop top and midi-skirt sets, hot pants,
flashy suits, jumpsuits, and sequins galore, modeled on tall, toned
women with long, flowing locks barrel-curled to perfection. A
smoky eye was commonplace, and everyone looked like they'd
just finished their final session of teeth whitening. Glamazons
well over six feet tall in heels effortlessly strutted to the buffet
line, and it felt like everyone was talking and laughing and having
the time of their lives. Each contestant was sugary sweet and
kind, but they were also immensely intimidating.

I scarfed down some eggs and fruit and quickly returned
to my room to practice a few mock onstage questions with my
mom over the phone before I started packing. I needed to fill one
bag to bring with me to rehearsal and the final competition, and
the rest of my bags would stay in the hotel room. I had to be

ready to go by 10 a.m. because after I left the room that morning, I wouldn't be back until after the competition. Or hopefully, if I won, I wouldn't be back at all.

The woman who won that night would move to a new hotel room—a sprawling suite at the end of the floor we were living on—and she wouldn't be moving her own stuff. Just after crowning, the contestant chaperones would go to her room and transport her luggage to the Miss USA suite so that immediately after the competition, she would already be under the care and control of a new director. Packing was a reminder that tonight was going to change someone's life.

I finished zipping my last bag just as I heard the knock I was expecting at the door. Taking another look around the room to make sure I wasn't forgetting anything, my eyes landed on my humble clump of mismatched luggage. I grinned a little, feeling like I'd finally made it to the finish line. I laid one of my "North Carolina" sashes across my luggage, so the chaperones would know which bags were mine, then plodded my way to the door while dragging my competition bag behind me.

There was a finality to leaving that room. I had a hotel key card in my bag, and I could certainly return if I'd forgotten something. But it simultaneously felt like I couldn't. It seemed as impossible as trying to travel back in time. Forward was the only way I could go.

● ● ●

During our final rehearsal, I was all adrenaline. I felt like I was walking on clouds and gazing down at life being played on fast-forward. The slow churn of the past two weeks had turned into a sprint as soon as the blinding stage lights blasted on and the music started. The celebrity hosts, Vanessa and Nick Lachey, came out and introduced the night's performer, T-Pain, who started into his medley of songs.

We practiced the opening dance number, along with the walking patterns for the swimsuit and evening gown portions of the show. Nick, who had dual hosting and talent duties, would be serenading us during the evening gown portion. A fake onstage question section came at lightning speed afterward, and all of a sudden we were clapping for the mock winner.

That was it. That was the last time we would be onstage until the judges were seated, the audience was screaming, and the cameras were all pointed at us.

We had a few hours before it was time to line up for the big show, so we all meandered into the backstage area where our dressing rooms were. Back at my station, I pulled on a soft pair of sweatpants and a robe and washed off my morning makeup, so I could reapply a fresh look for the televised event.

The energy backstage was light, almost jubilant. The dressing rooms were sectioned into several small areas, and I was in a room with about sixteen other contestants. One of the women was playing music on her phone, and some of us sang along to a few songs. We talked about how awestruck we were to have stood so close to the celebrities during rehearsal.

"I can't believe Madeleine actually touched him!" someone gleefully remarked. In our opening number, a small group of women were dancing in formation right behind T-Pain. Near the end of the dance section, Miss Mississippi USA was supposed to walk forward out of the formation and lean her arm on T-Pain's shoulder. It was like winning the choreography lottery.

We laughed and talked about how Miss Oklahoma USA, Triana, was in either the front or in another visible spot in every single dance number we had at the beginning of the show. And deservedly so. She was stunning and danced beautifully. I'd never seen her miss a pose. I really liked Triana and thought there was a good chance she'd be a front-runner.

I also thought Miss California USA and Miss Massachusetts USA were shoo-ins for the first cut. Erica had won the California title on her first try, not an easy feat for one of the largest and most competitive pageants in the country. She also worked for Google and frequently spoke about women in STEM (science, technology, engineering, and mathematics), a timely topic that I knew was being widely talked about. Kelly was a Harvard grad, twice over. She'd earned her undergraduate degree and master of business administration (MBA) and was doing executive coaching when she won the Massachusetts title. Also, both women were drop-dead gorgeous.

The stiff competition didn't end with them. The brilliant, talented, high-achieving women I was up against had started businesses and modeled all over the country. They'd raised tens of thousands of dollars for nonprofits and performed at Carnegie Hall. Although I was the lone practicing attorney, one woman had just graduated from law school and another was in her first year. There were makeup artists, a TV reporter, social workers, students, and women who'd advocated for body positivity, gender equality, and domestic violence awareness.

Regardless of my respect for my competitors, I refused to dwell on their accomplishments when I was at the competition. Each time my mind began to wander, I thought back to my own strengths or pulled out my notebook to review my notes on current events and possible onstage questions. I took comfort in my faith and knowing that, ultimately, it wasn't up to me. God had a plan, and my part of that plan was to prepare myself for the role as if I were going to win—and then let him take over after that.

At last, call time arrived.

I made the slow walk out of my dressing room, down the long hallway that led to the backstage area, and lined up behind Miss New York USA. By then, the audience had filed into the enormous theater, and I could hear the din created by thousands of people talking amongst themselves. The clock ticked closer to showtime.

In spite of my nervousness, standing in line and waiting to go onstage was one of the most blissful feelings I'd experienced during the entirety of the competition. There was a levity and carefree hopefulness in the air. Maybe it was the adrenaline pumping, or the relief that the moment had finally come, but just before the show started was when winning felt the most possible. The work was done. I'd sweated, stressed, and toiled for years on end, and all that was left was being present while it all unfolded.

• • •

My moment of bliss ended abruptly. Reality hit when I glanced over and saw one of the choreographers staring at a half sheet of paper she held in front of her. Her eyes were dashing between the line of contestants and the paper on which she was writing notes. We'd been placed into formations for a few different dance numbers, at the beginning of the show and before the swimsuit and evening gown portions. However, the women who advanced to finals would be removed from the dance numbers for the swimsuit and evening gown sections. There was no time for the finalists to dance in the swimsuit or evening gown performances and then get backstage into a line and immediately walk out on stage. The choreographers would have to rearrange our dance formations with the nonfinalist contestants, so they needed to know in advance who the finalists were.

This choreographer knew who had made the top fifteen. And who hadn't. I figured it wouldn't hurt to surreptitiously try to find out, just a few minutes before showtime.

Our "line" was more of a cluster, and tons of people were buzzing around backstage, so when I slyly walked away from the group, I went unnoticed. I made a large loop around the woman with the paper and ended up about twenty feet behind her. I figured I could nonchalantly walk past her and glance at the paper on my way back to my spot. As I approached, I could see that the paper had *X*'s arranged marking our formation for the swimsuit number, the first dance formation that would need to be changed. I could also see some markings underneath each *X*. I knew where I stood in the formation and as I walked past the woman, I felt like the air was being knocked out of my lungs. I thought I could make out the letter *N* underneath the *X* that designated my place in the formation. There was another letter after the *N* that I couldn't quite make out since the writing was so small and certainly meant to obstruct little spy-girl adventures like mine.

The room seemed to have gotten smaller, and I started to panic. *Oh my god. Ohmygod. Ohmygod . . . ohmygod . . . ohmygod. Oh. My. God. Did I not make finals?* I tried to convince myself that I hadn't just seen *NC* on the paper. If I was still in the dance, there was no way I'd made finals. But maybe it was actually *NJ*. Or *NY*. No, that wouldn't make sense—the letters didn't even look the same. Maybe that wasn't the new formation. Maybe they hadn't changed it yet.

In the midst of my self-inflicted freak-out session, I heard shouting close to the stage entrance. I looked over to see the production team waving my line onto the stage. Ready or not, it was time to take our places. I marched out with fifty other women to bright, flashing stage lights, more cameras than I could count, and a screaming audience while I slowly shook off my quiet hysteria and took my place at the front of the stage.

Chapter 2

ANYTHING COULD HAPPEN

Even though anxiety lingered in the back of my mind, I stood in my spot on the stage, smiling and searching the audience for my mom and stepdad as T-Pain walked up. The formation I was in for the opening number was front and center. The only person in front of our little group of about ten contestants was T-Pain himself. He took his place as the lights began to lower and I mentally said a prayer.

Your plan, God. Your plan.

The opening video package began to play on the two giant screens in the house of the theater, and the audience went crazy. The music started, and the competition began!

The bright and flashy opening number finished with hosts Vanessa and Nick standing center stage and all fifty-one contestants scattered onstage behind them. They ran through their brief opening dialogue before getting to the moment I'd been thinking about all day—the top fifteen announcement. I was barely balancing on my own two feet when they called the first state.

Florida.

She'd been on many pageant prediction lists, so I wasn't surprised. I had sat next to her a few times during rehearsal and liked her cool, laid-back persona.

Next up . . . New Mexico, another favorite.

Arkansas was third. A first-year law student and sure to be competitive if she advanced to the onstage question round.

Ohio. Then Oklahoma. Iowa came next, and Minnesota followed.

I was startled to hear the hosts announce that we would be moving to a commercial break. I looked over at the two lines of finalists and counted. Seven already. They were almost halfway finished, and I hadn't been called yet.

I started to sweat.

I began thinking about all the people at home who were watching and supporting me. People from my law firm. Friends from law school and undergrad. My dad, sister, and four little brothers.

Oh, God, please let me make it.

The commercial break ended, and we were back on deck. The stage was set up like a typical rectangle, but a wide runway split the middle and jutted out about twenty feet into the audience. All of the women who had not yet been called as finalists were standing on the back part of the stage on either side of the runway, and two cameramen were onstage with us. They flanked the runway, filming close-ups and reactions of each finalist who was announced. The other contestants and I had a vague idea of who would be called next because a cameraman would be standing close by, ready to zoom in on your face while you celebrated hearing your state called as you walked forward to join the other finalists.

Vanessa and Nick were about to call the eighth finalist, and a cameraman was hovering near me, his lens trained directly on my face. A wave of relief washed over me, and I flashed my best smile toward the camera. Nick began, "The next woman to make it to the top fifteen is . . . "

District of Columbia!

Miss DC, Cordelia, was standing in the row directly behind me, and I watched as, cameraman in tow, she walked to the front of the stage to join the group of finalists. I was happy for the eight women who had heard this spectacular news, but I was also dreading not making the cut. Each woman the hosts called brought me one step closer to that fear being realized.

The ninth finalist I couldn't help but celebrate. It was my lovely roommate, Victoria from Louisiana! She and I had the same state directors, so we'd spent a lot of time talking with each other, going to a few appearances together, and bonding before we arrived at the competition. I remember looking at her one day and saying, "I hope I end up in the top two, holding hands with you."

"Me too!" she said excitedly.

I found comfort in knowing that even if I didn't make it, at least Victoria was keeping up her side of our final-two bargain.

Nick was about to announce the tenth finalist. The suspenseful music began to play. "Still in the competition is . . . North Carolina!"

I could have lain down on the floor and cried. I took my place in line with the other finalists, barely able to stand still, exploding with jittery joy while the remaining five finalist announcements zipped by.

The other finalists and I filed offstage as the show cut to a commercial break. Like two giddy schoolgirls, Victoria and I ran to the separate backstage dressing room that had been designated for finalists. "Stop running!" someone yelled. We didn't care. We'd just landed two of the coveted top fifteen spots at Miss USA. We were unstoppable!

Most of us wore our bathing suit bottoms underneath our opening number outfits in order to save time when we needed to change. A few minutes after stepping foot backstage, I emerged from the dressing room with my swimsuit, earrings, and shoes on. I got in line and grabbed one of the sarongs we would be using during the competition. I wanted to make sure I could tie mine around my waist loosely enough to tug it off with one hand when I competed onstage but tightly enough that it wouldn't fall off as soon as I started walking. Backstage, I tied, removed, and retied the sarong over and over until it was my turn to walk onstage. Then I strutted out—hips swishing, smiling at the camera—and tugged at my sarong, ready to dramatically pull it off with one hand like I'd practiced.

It wouldn't budge.

I pulled a little harder and instead of falling open, the sarong slid higher up, past my belly button up to my rib cage. The rough fabric was catching on itself, making it difficult to pull open. I knew anyone watching could tell I was struggling.

I hadn't stopped walking while playing tug-of-war with my sarong, and by then I was well beyond the halfway point of the stage. Finally, I reached up with my other hand and shimmied the fabric apart.

"Ah, she got it!" Vanessa remarked when I finally won the battle with the piece of fabric I now despised.

The entire tussle lasted a few seconds, but it felt like a full minute. I didn't want anyone to feel sorry for me, though, and I refused to let the moment faze me. I smiled brighter, and as I reached my final mark, I decided to do a spin and a hair flip. I tossed my mane of curls like I was being featured in a shampoo commercial, eyed the camera, turned on my heel, and strutted back down the stage in my best attempt at a Naomi Campbell walk.

Once the top fifteen finished the swimsuit portion, it was time to announce who had made it to the top ten and would compete in evening gown. I was relieved to earn a spot despite my sarong debacle. Yet I was sad that Victoria didn't advance with me. The competition was tough, and I knew selecting who would move on was no easy task. But that didn't make it any less disappointing each time my friends were eliminated.

After a swift change, we were serenaded by Nick during the evening gown segment. I felt beautiful in my simple white, velvet, one-shoulder gown, with silver and gold beads draped around my shoulder and hanging down my back. I had wanted to wear something that wouldn't overpower my thick, curly hair and received just that with this dress, which had a smidge of sexiness due to a high slit on the left side.

The competition proceeded, and before I knew it, all ten of the finalists were lined up onstage again, shoulder to shoulder, holding hands and waiting to hear which of us would advance to the top five and the first of two live question rounds.

The favorite, Allie Gonzalez of New Mexico, was called into the top five first. She looked every bit like a national contender, gracefully moving to the front of the stage in an eye-catching yellow ball gown with a slit that showed off her long, slender legs. I'd prepared myself for getting called fourth or last, since I was consistently being called into each round late in the game, so my mouth hung open for a second and my feet wouldn't move after I was the next one called into the top five. *The top five at Miss USA!* I looked out into the audience and saw one of the production team members waving me forward. Nevada, Oklahoma, and Arkansas rounded out the final five.

I'd been practicing the onstage question portion of the competition every day for months. The difficulty in the onstage question is not just answering a tough question live in front of thousands of people in an auditorium and millions watching at home. It's in delivering a compelling, logical answer with a thirty-second time limit. One of my fears was reaching the time limit and hearing the "ding" noise that is supposed to be a pleasant reminder that your time is up but feels more like someone is telling you to shut the hell up. I'd overcompensated and practiced so much that I regularly finished my mock onstage questions in twenty-eight seconds without even having to look at a clock.

Another common fear is flubbing the onstage question and creating a negative viral moment. Several years before I competed in Miss USA, a Miss Teen USA contestant famously gave a garbled answer and afterward was bullied so harshly that she said she contemplated suicide. Many forget that she was only eighteen years old when she answered that question, volleyed by a panel of celebrity judges, into a mic in front of an audience of thousands, on a live television program broadcast to millions of viewers. People clam up and get nervous merely meeting a celebrity, let alone being surrounded by them while one of them asks you a question. I've seen adults forget their own names on live television when being interviewed by their local news station.

I told myself to let go of my nervousness and overthinking and focus on being in the moment onstage. *Just listen to the question, Cheslie.*

Allie walked to the mic first and drew lively applause while talking about the importance of the 2020 presidential election candidates addressing immigration. She strode back to her spot in line, smiling and projecting a deserved confidence.

"North Carolina, come on down."

I threw my shoulders back and told myself I was ready. Days before the competition, all fifty-one contestants had written questions for the top five finalists. Five nonfinalists were selected to read their questions live on the night of the television broadcast. The woman chosen to ask me the question she'd written was Miss Massachusetts USA. The double Harvard grad.

There I stood, across from one of the sharpest women in the competition. I knew she'd have a good question. Better yet, I knew I would be ready for it. I shut off the background noise in my brain and listened intently while she read her question from a card.

"For the past two years, the hashtags 'Me Too' and 'Time's Up' have dominated our conversation. However, some believe it has only deepened the divide between men and women. Have these movements gone too far?"

I took a moment and thought about what I wanted to say. When my mom and I had practiced onstage questions that morning, she'd told me to pause and gather my thoughts before I spoke, which seems obvious yet is quite scary to do. If someone puts a mic in your face, it feels awkward to stand there silently, even for a single second. But my practice answers were always better when I took the time to pause.

I heard Miss Massachusetts's question, and my knee-jerk reaction was, *No, of course they haven't.* Before I spoke, though, I considered why I believed that.

Why not, Cheslie? I thought to myself. *Why not?* And then it came to me: the true meaning behind the movements. Until we have equality, we haven't done enough. The purpose of #MeToo and #TimesUp was to demonstrate how pervasive sexual harassment was, especially in the workplace, and to do whatever it took to fix it. I was ready to give my response.

"I don't think these movements have gone too far," I said. "What 'Me Too' and 'Time's Up' are about are making sure that we foster safe and inclusive workplaces in our country. As an attorney, that's exactly what I want to hear, and that's exactly what I want for this country. I think they're good movements."

The applause started before I'd even finished my answer. The answer deserved all kinds of qualifiers and "except for when" examples and additional context, but I had thirty seconds, and I felt strongly about what I said, given the circumstances.

After listening to the remaining finalists' answers, I was confident about my chances of moving forward but knew that anything could happen, given the competition's inherent subjectivity. The commercial break was brief, and the announcement of the top three came quickly afterward.

"The first woman to make it to the top three is . . . "

"North Carolina!"

I'd made it!

Miss Oklahoma, Triana, and pageant favorite Allie from New Mexico completed the top three, advancing to the second round of onstage questioning.

"North Carolina, please join us," Vanessa said.

I walked to where she stood onstage after the top-three announcement, and she began to read the final question. I'd never listened so intently to anything in my entire life.

"Millennials are often labeled as entitled, but they've also been called one of the most socially conscious generations in decades. What is one word you would use to describe your generation, and why?"

She held the mic in front of my mouth as I stood silently. The first thought that came to mind was the progress our country was experiencing, especially in relation to gender equality. One week before finals night, all the contestants had visited the Nevada State Legislature, where we learned that the women lawmakers outnumbered the men. It was the first time that had happened in any state, and I remember feeling awestruck, sitting in a room listening to the voices of so many powerful women around me. Also, this had happened during a time when millennials made up almost a third of the voting-age population. It felt progressive and new and . . . well, innovative.

"I would say that my generation is innovative. I'm standing here in Nevada," I paused, making sure I referenced the milestone correctly before I went on, "in the state that has the first majority-female legislature in this entire country." The confidence and power in my voice reverberated throughout the auditorium.

The audience, sitting there in Nevada, went wild. I continued over their cheers.

"Mine is the first generation to have that forward-looking mindset that has inclusivity, diversity, and strength and empowered women. I'm looking forward to continued progress with my generation."

My strategy was to first answer the question, then add context and an explanation before finishing on a positive note. That's exactly how this answer came out, and for the first time in a while, I didn't pick apart my answer as soon as I walked away from the mic. I genuinely felt like it was my best response ever to a question I'd been given onstage during a competition.

· · ·

All that remained after that last question was the "final look," when the three finalists would have a chance to walk onstage solo. It's not technically scored, but we're told that the judges don't send in their ballots until after the final look.

The stage was set up beautifully, with lights everywhere. Lights built into the floor, lights on screens hanging in horizontal panes lining the entirety of the back of the stage, and a wide vertical pane of lights that started at the ceiling at the back of the stage and cascaded down to the floor, the base curving into the stage floor itself, like a giant slide connected to the back end of the stage runway.

In rehearsal, the final look began with the stage lights off, and when the music started, the large vertical pane and runway would slowly light up, starting at the middle and rolling outward. The transition from black to white looked like curtains opening to reveal blinding sunlight. It was a spectacular moment.

Since I had been the first contestant called into the final three, I took my place on the stage during the commercial break. I stood alone in darkness at the back of the monumental runway, the vertical pane at my back. The questions had been answered. I was happy with how I'd performed. All that was left was one more chance to slowly glide across the stage.

The hosts pulled everyone back from the commercial break and directed the viewers' attention to the stage as the lights started their dance, sliding the darkness away to reveal me standing by myself on the gargantuan stage, while the track for a gentle Dan + Shay ballad began to play: *You say you'll be down in five, the smell of your perfume.*

I took my first step forward.

Is floatin' down the stairs, you're fixin' up your hair like you do, the song continued.

The audience noise reached a thunderous peak. I levitated to the end of the runway and eased into a pose, facing the camera in front of me. The beads on my dress that hung from my shoulder and draped down to my hip swayed while I stood there, making me feel even more glamorous than I had when I'd whipped them around in the evening gown portion. I tried my best to hold on to the moment before it passed.

I blinked and suddenly, all fifty-one of us contestants were back onstage, preparing for Sarah Rose Summers to have her final walk as Miss USA 2018. The other two finalists and I were scattered on either side of the runway, onstage with the other contestants. While we waited for another commercial break to end, some of the nearby contestants congratulated me and wished me luck. I looked across the runway to the other side of the stage and made eye contact with Victoria. She'd been watching the pageant backstage with all the other contestants. She looked at me, nodded her head, and mouthed, *It's you.*

"Ladies, this is it," Vanessa said with finality. I was standing center stage next to Triana and Allie. We were about to hear the results, and I was in agony. Time stood still, and I barely had a harness on my nerves as each second crawled by.

"All three of you are so deserving of this honor, but as you know, there can only be one winner," Vanessa solemnly read from the teleprompter.

Don't say North Carolina. Don't say North Carolina, I repeated in my head. I started mentally saying the names of the other two contestants' states, hoping the hosts would follow suit.

"Oklahoma!"

Oh my God. Oh my God. Oh my God. Triana stepped forward out of line to accept her second runner-up flowers. I was so anxious I couldn't even clap. My hands were doing the motion, but no noise was coming out. I was numb. It was my turn to walk forward and hold hands with Miss New Mexico

USA, the woman so many pageant blogs had predicted to take the crown.

"Ladies, please make your way to center stage." The lights dimmed as we walked forward, turned to face each other, and lowered our heads. Out of the corner of my eye, I could see a cameraman on stage with us, circling around while we impatiently waited. Every light in the auditorium was off, except for one spotlight beaming down on Allie and me.

I felt an overwhelming sense of gratitude that God had brought me this far. I didn't want to lose, but if I did, I was at least glad I'd given a performance I was proud of. I closed my eyes and said a prayer out loud.

Dear God, thank you for this moment. Thank you for leading us this far. Please watch over our new Miss USA. Order her steps and lead her in the path you have designed. Amen.

I heard Vanessa's voice echoing in the auditorium: "And now, Miss USA 2019 is . . . "

Time stopped. This time I repeated my state name over and over again in my head, pleading for a win.

"*North Carolina!*"

The audience erupted, every light in the theater flashed on, and my knees gave out. I closed my eyes and squeezed Allie's hands, afraid to look out into the audience. I didn't want to wake up and realize I was dreaming. I'd dreamed of this scenario more than once, but my imagination never brought me past the winning announcement. I didn't know what was supposed to happen next.

I opened my eyes and saw Allie stepping away while a tall, slender woman with soft brown hair strode over to place a sash over my head. I thanked my new sister, Miss Universe, as Miss

Teen USA walked over and handed me a gigantic bouquet of flowers.

Turning, I stared blankly at the audience and blinked hard twice, still trying to figure out if I was dreaming. Instinctively, I squatted while Sarah placed a crown with two decades of history firmly onto my head. I stood and looked at her, not knowing what to do until she motioned toward the audience. In disbelief, I turned and walked forward.

The moment was mine.

I reached the end of the stage, raising my hand to wave at everyone and no one. Only a few seconds passed before I heard the rush of fifty contestants running toward me, covering me in hugs and warmth. Our bond truly was a sisterhood, and we were standing onstage celebrating together. Miss South Carolina, my neighboring state representative and friend, ran toward me so fast that she slipped and almost fell to the floor. Miss Texas reached up and straightened my crown. Victoria pushed through to squeeze my hand and congratulate me on capturing the title both of us had wanted so badly before she disappeared back into the crowd.

Chapter 3

ARE YOU READY?

For the people watching at home, the competition's craziness and suspense ends when the cameras turn off. For me, it was just getting started.

Since I'd arrived in Reno two weeks earlier, each moment of my life had been regimented, scheduled, and planned. I'd been told where to go and how long to stand there, and the other contestants and I had been through countless rehearsals. I don't remember any of us even asking what happens after you win. That part you figure out as you go.

Once the red light on the camera trained on me faded, a man in a black suit approached me and said, "I am your security. Come with me." I waved goodbye to my fellow contestants as he led me backstage, where a hair and makeup team descended upon me and feverishly started adjusting my crown, pinning my bangs back, powdering my face, and applying my lip gloss.

I did a brief on-camera interview with Miss Universe, Catriona Gray, on a small backstage set before being shuffled off to another area backstage, where I took my official Miss USA headshots. The organization would send these to all the media outlets covering the competition. No pressure.

A woman named Emily led me to each station, insisting, "We've gotta go, we've gotta go." We hurried back to the stage, where Emily pulled me toward a man wielding a microphone and a guy holding a large TV camera.

"Hi, we're from *Inside Edition*. Are you ready?"

After a short interview and photos onstage with my family, state pageant directors, pageant sponsors, the judges, the hosts, and T-Pain, Emily turned to me and told me it was time to head to the press conference. *Press conference?!* I thought. *How is this real life?* Emily led me, the security team, and the rest of our growing entourage down a set of stairs and out of the theater.

Barely twenty minutes into my reign, I'd done two interviews and two photoshoots and now was heading into my very own press conference. It was unreal. We walked out of the theater, which was connected to a casino, and through the bottom floor of the host hotel. The same security guard who'd pulled me from the stage ushered me through the mass of people in front of us. Everyone who'd watched the competition—including the contestants, their families and friends, state pageant directors, and pageant fans—lined the walkway. As I passed, they waved, cheered, and screamed "Congratulations!" A few chanted, "Cheslie, Cheslie, Cheslie!" It was a boisterous, joyful indoor parade.

We found an escalator and descended to one of the lower levels of the hotel, where the ballrooms were located. Security stood outside while Emily pushed me into a room. It was large and empty and, compared to the noisy celebration I'd just left, eerily quiet. A lone woman stood quietly, hands clasped in front of her. I immediately knew who she was, and as I walked up to her, I wasn't sure if I should introduce myself. Perhaps sensing my hesitance, she smiled and began speaking.

"Hello, I'm Paula Shugart." The president of the Miss Universe Organization.

Paula congratulated me and extended a few additional pleasantries. She explained that she would be introducing me at the press conference and asked if I was ready.

"Ready as I'll ever be!" I said.

We walked to an adjoining room that contained an elevated stage with a huge backdrop. Rows of chairs faced the stage, and a sizable group of journalists were sitting on and standing around the chairs. After Paula introduced me, I stepped onto the stage to answer a volley of questions from the press.

The next stop was my final one. Emily, our security detail, and another woman I hadn't yet met led me to an upstairs suite in the hotel. The winner's suite. *My* suite.

I asked Emily when I'd be able to see my family, and she told me they'd be waiting for me. Sure enough, we were twenty feet away from the suite when my directors threw the doors open and my family and friends spilled out. I shrieked and started a round of hugs. Emily and the new woman told everyone they needed to talk to me, my family, and my state directors alone in the suite before we could relax and celebrate.

Oh no, have I messed up already? I wondered.

Everyone cleared out and stood in the hallway, while I sat at one end of a long table in the dining area of the suite. The new woman stood at the opposite end of the table and introduced herself.

"My name is Esther Swan, and I'm the director of talent for the Miss Universe Organization."

My mom, stepdad, boyfriend, and directors lined the table and a nearby couch. We listened as Esther began to talk about my schedule for the next few days. I needed to pack my bags and be ready for a 4:30 a.m. car that would take us to the airport. I would move into my new apartment in Manhattan the next day and spend the weekend doing media training at the office and having fittings with the MUO stylist. *A stylist!* On Monday, I'd begin a media tour, and a hair and makeup team (*a team!*) would meet me each morning to ready me for the week.

Esther told me that life was going to be different moving forward. People would want to know me, follow me, contact me. "I'm sure your Instagram followers have already blown up."

"Where is my phone?!" I asked.

I stood up, and Esther laughed and motioned toward the bedroom, where the chaperones had dropped off everything from my previous hotel room and had also retrieved the bag I'd brought to the theater. I went into the room and dug my phone out of one of the bags. Returning to the table while unlocking my phone, I checked the follower count on my personal Instagram page. Sure enough, my followers were nearing the forty thousand mark and counting—more than double what I'd had a few hours before and a fraction of what I'd have by the end of my reign.

I set my phone down and turned my attention back to Esther. She told us to hang out as long as we wanted and order room service if we liked. Then she and Emily left, and my friends who'd been waiting in the hallway entered the room.

I browsed through the room service menu and ordered everything that sounded remotely tasty. Soon enough, a server wheeled an entire cart up to the room, with pasta, pizza, a milkshake, and a few other desserts and entrees. Someone turned the television on and flipped to the pageant. We were two hours behind the East Coast broadcast, so we got to rewatch the tape-delayed coverage. Everyone relayed their favorite moments and gave me a play-by-play of the thoughts they were having during the competition. It was exciting to hear their perspectives and relive the moments all over again.

My stepdad was talking and scrolling on his phone when he looked up at me and said, "*USA Today* wrote an article about you."

My eyes grew wide.

"What?!" I said in disbelief. He handed me his phone, and I skimmed through the piece. It had been barely an hour since I'd won. How could they have already written about me?

I pulled out my own phone, and when I googled my name, my mouth dropped open when I saw the number of articles that had already been posted.

"Miss USA 2019: 5 Things to Know About Miss North Carolina Cheslie Kryst."

"Read the Miss USA pageant Q&A segment, which involved politics and the Me Too movement."

"Miss USA: 5 Things You Missed During the Pageant."

They were writing about the number of degrees I had and from which schools I'd earned them. They knew I was licensed to practice law in two states. They knew which law firm I worked for and posted about me being the oldest woman ever to win the title. They'd reposted photos and captions from my personal Instagram page and talked about my fashion blog. It was overwhelming for a girl who used to delight in cutting out and saving clippings from anytime her name was listed beside my long jump mark—coverage that was usually buried in the back of the local newspaper's weekly sports roundup. Now I was reading national news outlet articles and their take on my win. One of my favorite news headlines that appeared shortly after my win read: "Miss USA Can Sue You."

As the night waned and my friends and family trickled out of the room, I kicked back to check my Instagram page again and scroll through messages and stories posted by friends and family and countless people I didn't know. One celebrity asked if I would defend a close friend of hers who had been charged with murder. Others were congratulating me and posting my photo everywhere. That's when I saw some collages that placed my photo alongside those of two other titleholders that year: Kaliegh Garris, who had won Miss Teen USA just a few days prior, and my friend and client Nia Franklin, who had won Miss America.

It dawned on me that all three of us winning meant that three women of color simultaneously held three well-known national pageant titles at the same time. I didn't think that had happened before, and I could barely comprehend its importance at nearly three o'clock in the morning. That night, I couldn't have known that I would spend much of my reign talking about the significance of Black women holding numerous prestigious pageant titles in the same year.

Chapter 4

NEVER ENOUGH

The Saturday after the competition, I woke up in a guilt-ridden panic. The sinking feeling in the pit of my stomach wasn't just dread—it was the Reese's Pieces, Twizzlers, and bagels I'd been shoveling into my mouth the day before.

Why do you do this? I softly chided myself, eyes still closed. All I could think about was the impending swimsuit competition and the months of battling my notorious sweet tooth that had been wasted on a ridiculous sugar binge.

Swimsuit was my favorite phase of competition in pageantry, and I prided myself on my body of work. As my heart rate began to quicken, I started mentally mapping out what kind of workout I would need to do to burn off the sugary calories and guilt—and then I opened my eyes and saw her.

A few feet away from me, on a worn brown dresser that seemed oddly familiar, sat the glittering $200,000 pearl-and-diamond prize: the Miss USA Mikimoto crown. The realization slowly dawned on me as my early-morning brain fog began to fade.

I won.

I slumped back with relief into the pillows on the comfy bed I would call mine for the duration of my reign and slowly panned the room that was starting to brighten in the break of day. Bare, pale-blue walls that I couldn't wait to decorate. A large window overlooking a street that was already crowded with angry cars and loud people at barely six o'clock in the morning. Two separate doors hiding what would become my walk-in closet and my shoe closet, respectively. This was the room that every Miss USA for over a decade had lived in—nestled in a Manhattan high-rise, feeling like the world was at her feet.

I'd spent the entire Friday prior traveling and eating junk food at various airports, hence the chocolate and candy. I traveled with my new manager, the Director of Talent for the Miss Universe Organization, and my new roommate, Miss Universe herself. I went from never having met Catriona Gray—who was legitimately famous in her home country, the Philippines—to living in a room one door down from hers.

"Overnight success" is a common phrase, but it is rarely used literally because there are few nights that truly snatch you from the life you knew into a new one. I can tell you from experience that winning Miss USA warranted a bit of confusion the morning after arriving in a completely different world.

I was still wearing my stage makeup on the two planes I took to get to New York City, the place I'd call home for the duration of my reign. On the first plane I bought an internet package, so I could download photos from the night before and read more of the steady stream of articles popping up online. The amount of information that journalists were finding out about me was staggering. And it had been barely half a day since the pearls and diamonds were placed on my head.

The Miss USA competition had happened on a Thursday night, which meant I had the weekend to pull myself together and prepare for interviews given by some of the largest media outlets in the world, beginning on Monday morning. *Good Morning*

America, Live with Kelly and Ryan, CBS This Morning, TMZ, FOX, AOL BUILD, and others were expecting to see me in person.

And imagine that just a few days earlier, I had repaired one of my acrylic nails with superglue from a general store at the casino, after it had cracked off in rehearsal.

My nails weren't the only detail to manage. I had more than a few items to cross off my to-do list before giving some of the most important interviews of my life. For starters, I needed to buy new underwear. I had brought enough for the two weeks I was at the competition, but I'd sent a giant suitcase home to North Carolina with my mom, full of all the dirty clothes I'd worn. I didn't think to bring my underwear with me and wash it after I arrived in New York. The pair I had on and my one extra pair obviously wouldn't last long.

I woke up early on Saturday to go buy the underwear I needed. I considered asking Catriona to recommend some places to me, but in spite of being a little intimidated, I figured I'd set out on my own. Really, who asks Miss Universe for underwear recommendations? I'd only spent a few hours with her and didn't yet know her as my roommate "Cat." At that point, I only knew her as the winner of the most sought-after title in the world. I crept out of our apartment as quietly as I could and started my journey.

Once I was out on my own in my new city, I realized the wild storm of emotions swirling inside me. There was a combination of excitement and nervousness about being in this brand-new place. Joy mixed with disbelief that I'd earned my dream job, and a bit of anxiety meshed with confusion that I hadn't yet straightened out in my head. On top of that, layer the "get-out-of-my-face" directness New Yorkers seemed to have, and basically, I was crying about everything.

I don't fancy myself a crier. As a young attorney, I was used to having people question my work, argue with me in court, and constantly try to prove me wrong. I had fairly thick skin, but in New York City, it felt like every response from a sales associate was tinged with a certain "What do you want?" tone, and each time I spoke, their facial expressions seemed to convey that I wasn't talking fast enough.

"Can I help you find anything?" the store greeter asked, as if she were demanding a game-show quick answer.

I told her what I was looking for, and she motioned to a nearby escalator. "Upstairs."

Before I could thank her, she was already moving toward another person who'd walked through the doors behind me.

After buying enough underwear to last several weeks, my next stop was a nail salon a few blocks away, which had acrylics listed on their website. Once I arrived, I learned that only one person in the salon had an inkling of an idea how to do acrylic nails, and I was surprised to see she didn't have any of the typical electric tools on hand. Two hours later, my nails were visibly uneven, and my cuticles were bloody fragments thanks to how she'd scratched them with her imprecise nail file. Relieved to have survived the painful process, I walked to the counter to pay.

"How much?" I asked as I whipped out my credit card.

"Eighty dollars."

I paused in disbelief. That was twice the price I would've paid back home. I had plain nude nail polish without any fancy designs or artwork, and nothing about my nails was done right. Although the Miss Universe Organization would reimburse me for all my nail appointments, in good conscience, I couldn't bring an eighty-dollar nail appointment receipt to my boss. *Lord Jesus*, I thought, *I'm being scammed already.*

"Eighty dollars? Why does it cost so much?" After a couple minutes of back and forth, I decided to just pay and leave. I was more afraid of causing too big of a stir and ending up in a random, skeezy tabloid than I was of having someone at MUO be upset about the cost. I could see the pending headline: "New Miss USA Stiffs Small Business for Nail Bill." How was I messing up this badly already?

The real test, though, would come at my styling appointment.

One perk of being Miss USA is that MUO provides a stylist to help dress us for appearances and events. It was one of the reasons I'd felt comfortable sending home most of the clothes I'd brought to the competition. I was going to get new ones in the Big Apple!

When I arrived at my meeting with the stylist at the Miss Universe offices, I walked past the lobby, turned left, and stepped into a windowless room about twelve feet long and seven feet wide. A petite woman with glasses and blonde hair past her shoulders stood inside the room, talking to a young woman who I assumed was her assistant. The stylist looked exactly as I'd expected—unique, edgy, adventurous even. Her British accent made everything she said sound stylish.

More important, though, than the stylist and the room were the two racks of clothing for me to look through, which spanned the entire length of one wall. Before reaching for the rack, the stylist asked if we could sit down to discuss my personal style. I was glad to know she cared to ask rather than diving right in with a bunch of clothes I was unsure about.

We walked to the lone conference room positioned at the back corner of the floor and pushed through the luxe glass doors. A massive white, square table large enough to seat more than a dozen people separated us from the sprawling, panoramic view of midtown New York City. It was a daunting room, but the perfect setting to talk about fashion.

"Who is your style inspiration?" the stylist asked.

"Oh, easy! Olivia Pope from *Scandal.*"

Her brow furrowed a bit and she looked at me quizzically.

I idolized the Olivia Pope character, the Georgetown Law–educated attorney who no longer practiced law but operated as a DC-based "fixer" and was an international boss not to be trifled with. As an attorney, I identified with her views as a feminist and her challenges as a Black woman who knew what every Black professional (and indeed every Black child) knows: you have to be twice as good to get half of what others have.

And I loved Olivia Pope's wardrobe, full of eye-catching, soft, classic silhouettes and colors. She always looked powerful, strutting into scenes in fabulous coats, suits, and dresses, even rocking gloves past her elbows on occasion. So, of course I wanted to dress like her. I'd even written about her on my fashion blog for women's work clothing, *White Collar Glam.*

But Olivia Pope wasn't Miss USA. I realized only in hindsight that Olivia operated in our nation's capital, where suits belonged and cleavage didn't. I would need a different type of wardrobe for when I threw out the first pitch at a baseball game or announced the winner of the World's Strongest Man Competition.

"Do you have any others?" the stylist quizzed me, smiling kindly as she asked.

I didn't.

Pulling up my Pinterest account on my phone, I scrolled through some pictures I'd organized into folders as outfit inspirations. True to form, the photos were of women in suits, button-down blouses, slacks, and pencil skirts, all devoid of patterns and bright colors.

"I really feel comfortable wearing suits." I was trying to keep my voice from cracking. "I think you can wear them in a lot of different settings, and they're really versatile, especially now when suit-inspired outfits are trendy as casual wear."

"Why don't we go back to the rack and take a look at what we have there? Try a few things on?"

We backtracked to the styling room and the racks stuffed with clothing. As I began more closely examining the items available to me, I was almost insulted. Nothing screamed my name. The stylist had assembled an exquisite, versatile assortment of clothes in various styles and sizes. Since she'd had no idea who the winner would be, she had attempted to whip together a plethora of options that would work for anybody. Unfortunately, she was now working with a close-minded woman who wasn't willing to experiment and had echoes of "you didn't deserve to win" ringing in her ears. All I could see were frilly, floral-patterned dresses, blouses with prints I didn't like, and other casual pieces that were a far cry from what I was used to wearing. Did they think I was some country bumpkin who'd arrived in the big city straight from the sticks? Where were the suits?

I fell quiet, and the awkward silence of the room was deafening. She offered outfits, and I reluctantly tried them on. My mirror image seemingly teased me, sneering, *You're a failure*.

Trying to find some common ground, I gingerly tugged my phone out of my purse again and flipped through some photos of outfits I'd worn at Miss USA, hoping to offer the stylist a better feel of my fashion sense and what I felt comfortable wearing.

More silence.

It took all the energy I had left to prevent the tears welling up in my eyes from falling down my cheeks. I had worn all my favorite outfits at the competition and then sent them home.

Would I have to wear my castaway emergency options to meet Kelly Ripa and Ryan Seacrest and Gayle King on national television? Plus, I had a meeting with a media consultant and a few other appearances scheduled on my calendar for the very next day, and I had no time to go shop for anything myself.

After making a few more attempts to choose suitable outfits from the rack, my throat started to close while I tried to keep my lips from quivering and refrain from melting into hysterics.

The stylist finally turned to me and asked, "Where do you like to shop?"

"Zara."

"If you could wear anything from Zara, what would you wear?"

Her grace and resilience made me feel worse. I felt like a bad person both for not being able to hold it together and for not loving what she'd worked so hard to assemble.

We agreed that I would go home, screenshot a few items from Zara that I wanted to wear, and send the pictures to her. I trudged back to the titleholder apartment, and after finally reaching the safety of solitude in my room, bawled my eyes out as quietly as I could, hoping Miss Universe couldn't hear me from the next room.

I felt guilty sobbing over fingernails, clothes, money that was going to be refunded, and someone not smiling at me in a store. These trivial trials stabbed at a deep insecurity I carried—the unshakable feeling that I did not belong. I struggled with thinking I wasn't good enough for the role I'd earned, that I would never measure up to the perfection I assumed the other fifty contestants were capable of and would have displayed if given the chance. The constant inner voice repeating "never enough" was compounded by the treatment from the world seeming to confirm my fear.

Online, there were exponentially more positive comments than negative ones, and while it's not a surprise that the internet drags out the nasty in some people, the near-constant barrage of online attacks I read felt very personal.

Praying for her reign to finish ASAP.

Man body.

Miss New Mexico should have won!!

Seriously, didn't they have anyone else to give that crown? It should be beauty with brains. Not just brains alone.

Only need to do a facial harmonization and a rhinoplasty.

The only people that "think" she was the most beautiful are the Black women.

Just hours after my win, I had to delete vomit-face emojis that a few accounts had plastered all over the comments on my Instagram page. More than one person messaged me telling me to kill myself. All of this only added to my long-standing insecurities—the feeling that everyone around me knew more than I did, that everyone else was better at my job, and that I didn't deserve this title. People would soon find out I was a fraud. I felt like an impostor, but not just in pageants.

• • •

As a standout student in the seventh grade, I was selected to be part of a program that had kids take the SAT early. Without even studying, I managed to score a 1010 out of 1600 at barely twelve years old. This achievement garnered the attention of a college in Virginia, and although the program would have allowed me to graduate with a college degree at age eighteen, I opted to pass up that opportunity and attend regular high school instead. I thrived as a big fish in a little pond, and by the time I graduated,

I'd been Miss Fort Mill High, prom queen, captain of the varsity cheerleading team twice, captain of the track team, and president of the Beta Club. I'd also picked up a couple of AP courses and earned admission into the only school I'd applied to, the Honors College at the University of South Carolina.

My undergrad years proved to be a fun, low-pressure environment, but everything flipped when I entered law school and business school. As I started learning about the career of my dreams, I learned another lesson: I was nothing special. Everyone I met was extraordinary. I was attending classes with valedictorians, athletes, and Ivy League grads, along with former working professionals with several degrees already under their belts. These were people who'd traveled the world, had plans to change it, and were willing to put in the work every night at the library to do it.

My competitive spirit helped initially with the dual-degree program that would allow me to earn my law degree and my MBA at the same time. I started my first year strong, but eventually, my motivation wore thin as I split my focus between law school and business school and generally having a good time during my last few years as a student. And it showed.

One day, as I sat among my classmates in my least favorite class, my professor asked me a question that I then answered correctly.

"See! You are smart," he said.

I was shocked and embarrassed. I'd never communicated my concerns about whether I belonged, and I always made decent grades. Did he mean he thought I was stupid?

To my horror, a classmate of mine continued the dialogue.

"What do you mean? Are you trying to say you don't think she's smart?" she demanded.

I liked this classmate and knew she meant well by trying to point out the audacity of the professor's statement, but I wanted to physically melt into the floor. In response, he rattled off some reason for his comment. Yet I felt attacked and said nothing, hoping we could just move on as quickly as possible.

I relive and feel moments such as these far more intensely and more often than I remember my wins.

The best strategy I learned for getting through and pushing past those moments when I doubted myself was simply to go do it—whatever "it" was. Impostor syndrome speaks to your inner fear and feeds your doubt. It questions your sanity and confidence. It tells you that you aren't good enough, that everyone else has it figured out, and that you should quit. I found that even when I felt inadequate, just showing up was a victory. Inserting myself into a space I thought I didn't belong and giving my all was my power. It would've been easy to turn away and accept defeat, but I chose the challenge.

Still, the more I showed up, the more I saw cracks in a foundation I'd previously thought was impenetrable. I saw firsthand that very few people really know what they're doing, and nobody has all the answers. The embarrassing moments I experienced weren't always unique to me, even if I never saw them happen to others.

I was grateful that my competitive nature and a little adrenaline allowed me to compartmentalize in high-pressure situations. In law school competitions, business school presentations, and pageants, I was able to suppress my feelings of doubt and focus solely on the task at hand. It happened intentionally and systematically. I'd used this very strategy at Miss USA.

I'd thought I'd performed poorly in the interview portion of the competition, which is the first chance the judges get to see the contestants in person, and the only chance they get to talk to us. I don't remember all of my responses, but I vividly recall writing about it in my pageant notebook two days before the competition:

> I didn't feel strong about interview on Monday. In fact, I felt like I blew it. I was sad all day . . . I was distracted in rehearsal. And now I'm done. I don't care how I messed up. I don't care what anyone thinks, I don't give a s***. The only thing I need to worry about is staying focused and prepared to win. If it's in God's plan for me to win, I will. And if it's not in God's plan for me, there's nothing I can do to change it. I'm ready.

After writing those words, I closed the notebook and put my doubts about the interview out of my mind. Over the next couple of days, each time any negative thought about it surfaced, I redirected myself to practicing positivity and focusing on my own preparedness. When I walked onto the stage the night of the competition, I didn't think about whether I'd done well in the interview, whether I'd done enough sit-ups to feel good in my swimsuit, or whether my dress was the right selection. I thought only of the task at hand.

Regardless of whether I felt deserving of my new title after I won or loved the new clothes I tried on, how much my nails cost the organization or whether salespeople in New York smiled at me, I was going to show up come media week.

As promised, by Monday morning the stylist found and delivered some of the Zara outfits I'd selected and added in some additional pieces. Each outfit fell well within my narrow comfort zone. I felt unstoppable when I left my apartment and climbed into a waiting SUV, which already carried three women from MUO in it.

Jackie Shahinian was the director of public relations for the organization, and she sat between one of the marketing and business development leads and the lead digital producer. They accompanied me to every interview, took photos, checked my hair and makeup, carried my extra clothes, and helped me throughout the day. I didn't have to figure out where each interview was or reach out to some unknown contact once I arrived. They handled everything for me. Showing up with a team made me feel like a star and helped me feel like a winner.

When we arrived at *Live with Kelly and Ryan* and it was time for me to walk on set, I strutted out in a blood-orange, long-sleeved, A-line dress that stopped a few inches above my knee. It had a ruffle detail from the shoulders to my wrists and another at the hem of the dress that felt playful but not juvenile. On camera, I hugged Ryan and elbow-bumped Kelly, who was sick at the time. I then perched atop a high chair, legs crossed at the ankle, feeling at ease.

"Has it sunk in?" Kelly asked.

"It hasn't! Every day I wake up and I'm like gah, I ate so many sweets yesterday. I have to compete in swimsuit tomorrow. And then I think oh, no, I won."

The audience laughed at my little quip, and I earned a chuckle from Kelly and Ryan too. They were easy to talk to and even when they weren't smiling, each of them had their own genial aura that made me feel like we'd been friends for years. For a few minutes, I forgot about the cameras, imagining that the audience was a group of friends gathered around a lunchroom table, and I believed that the Miss USA sash belonged right where it was.

• • •

Over the next few weeks, the media coverage and interviews continued. I almost always suppressed my panicky thoughts and feelings of inadequacy during my interviews. I only felt like a failure afterward, as I meticulously picked apart each of my responses and kicked myself for not using a better word or saying a profound phrase or interjecting humor or throwing out a useful stat. It was rare that I felt I'd truly nailed an interview. I wondered if I was frustrating Jackie, who would ask me how I felt after each interview, only to have me respond, "It was okay."

Being in a new job in a new city with an unpredictable schedule exacerbated my impostor feelings. Day-to-day I had a different agenda and was meeting tons of new people, which was a bit nightmarish for an introvert who relied on routine and whose social energy tank would drain down to empty each day. I felt scatterbrained some days, still waking up not knowing where I was and having to recalibrate each morning. The unsteadiness soon began to wear on me in more tangible ways.

My general feeling of confusion and absentmindedness, which I hoped my new employer didn't notice, devolved into forgetfulness that was hard to miss. When I'd moved to New York, I'd brought two cell phones with me—a personal phone and one provided by my law firm for work. A week into my reign, MUO gave me what became my third cell phone, strictly for Miss Universe communication and emails. I received it right before hopping into a chauffeured car to head to the airport for some events back home in Charlotte. Since I didn't have space in my purse for the box containing the new cell phone, I carried it separately, too afraid to throw it into my suitcase. Once I boarded the plane, I reached for the phone box to see if it was charged enough for me to turn it on and begin the setup process.

Where was it?

I remembered putting my purse on the ground and pushing it under my seat on the plane. Maybe the box was behind my purse. I tugged the purse out from under my seat and put it in my lap. I then reached back under the seat, to no avail.

Maybe I had actually squeezed the phone box into my purse and didn't remember doing so? I dug my hand into my bag, starting to grow a little frantic as I confirmed that the box wasn't there.

Did I leave it in the car? Did it even make it to the airport? Did I drop it on the ground when I was walking to the gate? My name was printed on the box's label in tiny letters. Had someone swiped the box, intent on hacking into the MUO system? What had I done?

Now in full panic mode, I hoped I could locate the phone before the flight attendants shut the plane door and told me to turn my phone on airplane mode. I texted the driver who had dropped me off and asked if the box was still in the back seat. He replied immediately, saying he didn't have it.

I started to sweat, wondering how much money it would cost to replace the phone and how much trouble I would be in for having lost the phone within an hour of receiving it. While my thoughts raced, a flight attendant with a kind face stopped at my row and leaned toward me.

"Hey, did you lose a cell phone?" she asked.

Lord, how does everyone already know? I thought.

"Yes, actually." I exhaled, a bit confused.

"You're Cheslie Kryst, right?"

"Yes."

"You left it at check-in—they're bringing it here now."

I could have cried from joy and relief. Thanking the attendant profusely, I slid back into my seat. As soon as the phone was back in my possession, I didn't let it out of my sight after that, carrying it on my lap the whole plane ride.

The absentmindedness didn't stop there. I left the keys to my new apartment in New York inside my old apartment in Charlotte. More than once, I arrived at an interview without my Miss USA sash. And I'd flat-out given up on learning the names of anyone new I met, besides people in the Miss Universe office and the doormen in my building.

Winning Miss USA hadn't made my imposter syndrome go away. Instead, I was waiting for people to realize I didn't have a clue about what I was doing. I'd perfected how to deal with that feeling in competition or in small doses—I could compartmentalize anything in short bursts. My approach to my imposter syndrome was all about distraction. I'd immediately focus my thoughts on positive statements of power, but that only lasted for so long. I needed to figure out how to deal with imposter syndrome when it crept up in everyday life—in the mundane moments after a performance, competition, or interview.

The other part of my solution was unadulterated audacity. I realized my feelings of inadequacy were typically outward facing. I compared myself to other titleholders, other attorneys at my firm, and other public figures I thought were flawless. The qualities I thought demonstrated that I didn't fit in were the qualities that made me unique, special, and powerful. That realization inspired a nerve, a courageous gall I rarely felt and almost always suppressed.

For example, it's difficult being in rooms and sitting on leadership boards where you are the only Black person, the only woman, and the youngest individual. Times like that used to feed my imposter syndrome, making me think I had to be perfect because I had to represent for all youth, women, and Black people who also wanted to be in the room but had been denied access.

In other instances, I felt as though I had a target on my back, like everyone was watching me or believed that the only reason I was in those rooms was by some stroke of luck. The hurdles I had to leap over, the obstacle courses I had to conquer just to reach another day, sharpened me and made me more qualified and ready than many of the people I sat amongst.

As a young attorney, I had to prepare twice as much as older attorneys to convince my client that I was knowledgeable and experienced enough to represent them. At the courthouse door, I had to whip out my bar card to show security that yes, I was an attorney, and I was therefore allowed to bring in my laptop and cell phone. I had to code switch once I stood in front of the judge to argue for my client, and I had to do it with a smile on my face, so I wouldn't fit the angry Black woman stereotype—being regarded as "nice" and "well-liked" was key to my success. I had to flex more strategic muscles every day than many others, and doing that made me stronger, smarter, more self-aware. This all forced me to be well-prepared, because anything less than excellence wouldn't get me in the door.

Over time, I thought back to those moments when I felt excluded, and I slowly began to realize that being the only one who looks like you is not a demonstration of why you don't belong—it shows why you *do* belong. My presence alone in spaces where other people don't look like me demonstrates my worthiness to be there.

Little by little, I began to reassess why I felt unworthy, realizing that I needed to understand that what I thought was a show of unworthiness was actually a demonstration of undeniable strength. The personal attacks I was fielding on social media got easier to handle when it occurred to me that if I hadn't won Miss USA, those trolls wouldn't notice me at all. The cyberbullying came with the job I'd worked for, stressed for, and earned, which meant that I'd already endured a fair amount of challenge on the way to my win. People I respected—the judging panel—had thought me worthy for the position. Although I was never able to totally ignore the mean, angry comments, the perspective I built significantly dulled the sting. (So did knowing that those bullies must have had awful lives if they thought the best use of their time was spending it spewing hatred on the internet.)

While testing out my changing perspective in my day-to-day life, I maintained my same pluckiness for high-adrenaline events. One of those events was a celebrity flag football game hosted by a nonprofit that partnered with MUO. I thought I'd be allowed to watch from the sidelines, but soon found out I'd be playing in the game, which included numerous professional football players and featured Tom Brady at the quarterback position. Yes, I was supposed to play flag football on the same field as one of the greatest football players of all time.

One of the event organizers pointed out the fact that I was a former Division I track and field athlete and said I would be great in the game. My immediate reaction was, *Yes, I was a college athlete, but I'm six years removed from that intense training, and even then, I never had to catch anything while I was running.* Instead of beating myself up and allowing my doubt and fear of embarrassment to make me feel like I didn't belong, I changed my thoughts to, *Yes, I'm a former college athlete, and they're all about to see how great I am, even six years out.*

My approach paid off. On one play, I scrambled over to someone running with the ball, pushed them out of bounds, caught their flag on fourth down, and forced a turnover. As my team started jogging down the field, about to switch sides, Tom Brady pointed at me and shouted down the field, "Good defense!"

You couldn't tell me a damn thing the rest of the day.

Chapter 5

WHY OUR WINS MATTERED

In 2002, eleven years before the Mikimoto crown was placed on my head, I was sitting in the audience next to my dad and siblings the night my mom became the second Black woman in history to win Mrs. North Carolina US, a pageant for married women. By the next day, everyone in our cul-de-sac at home knew about her win, and kids at school were asking me for autograph cards signed by my mom. Watching her win made me want to compete in pageants and taught me that Black women *could* win. However, life taught me that it was easier said than done.

I won the first pageant I ever competed in, becoming Miss Freshman at a school in Rock Hill, South Carolina. The letters on my sash peeled off a few months after my win; they'd been drawn onto a roll of sash paper with a glitter glue pen. The crown yellowed and fell apart after being exposed to too much sunlight while on display in my room. But man, I felt special each time I looked at that crown and sash, and I cherished both of those mementos like I'd never see anything like them again. I didn't care what condition they ended up in. I warmed with pride every time I gazed at them. And I wanted more.

After my family moved to Tega Cay, South Carolina, the next year, I competed a couple more times, winning the overall Miss

Fort Mill High School title my senior year. When I started college, I was overwhelmed with schoolwork, track and field training, and a job, so I didn't compete again until I was in law school. Looking back, it's somewhat comical that I convinced myself to jump back into the world of pageantry in law school, because I thought I'd have more time than I'd had as an undergrad. But jump I did, into a unique community very few people in this country have experienced or truly understand.

Law school and graduate programs don't typically have school pageants, so it was time for me to look elsewhere. A Google search led me to a local pageant in the Miss America system, even though I'd only ever watched one local competition. I knew the distinction between MUO (Miss Universe Organization) and MAO (Miss America Organization)—primarily that Miss America had a talent phase of competition and awarded scholarships, while Donald Trump owned Miss Universe, and it had gained a reputation for being the sexy and glamorous, albeit controversial, system. I understood that people still thought pageants were misogynistic, so I figured that if any law firm I interned or worked for took issue with me competing, I could argue that Miss America was the squeaky-clean system in which you'd want an attorney involved.

In order to compete at Miss North Carolina, which was the state I qualified for given my status as a student at Wake Forest, I had to win a local competition. It took competing in three different locals for me to win a title, and it was probably because they gave out three crowns that night. I wore a cheap swimsuit I'd sewn rhinestones onto and a black velvet evening gown I'd borrowed from my mom. For the talent portion, I played piano in a white tuxedo jacket with tails, a black vest, and white pants that were about five inches too short. Nevertheless, I won and punched my ticket to the next phase.

After taking pictures onstage with the other two winners, I was ushered backstage to a room to get some feedback from the judges and talk to the local director. I was overjoyed just to be carrying some flowers, and I kept looking down at the sash across my chest, its red lettering beautifully sewn onto thick white fabric draped over my shoulder and around one of my hips. This was a long way from the glitter glue sash I'd won when I was fourteen. I don't remember a word the judges said, and I'm sure they could sense my excitement and naïvete.

The one comment from that night I never will forget, though, came from the local pageant director. As I walked out of the room, she looked at me squarely in the face, her eyes narrowing a bit when she said, "You don't have any idea what you just got yourself into, do you?"

I didn't.

A few weeks later, I found out what she meant. The North Carolina officials held "Work Weekend," a multiday conference that all titleholders were required to attend. We turned in paperwork, tried on and purchased opening number outfits, took group photos, sat through meetings with the reigning Miss North Carolina and the state director, and had a chance to get to know each other. My mom was with me to witness this experience, which was unlike anything we'd ever seen before.

People frequently say women who compete in pageants are fake, and I began to see why. The exchanges that soon became familiar to my mom and me weren't much different from average office politics, but I also needed to learn pageant language. It felt like everyone else was speaking Latin. It also felt like everyone already knew each other and understood what was happening and why. Moreover, between Work Weekend and the pageant itself, I kept hearing the same phrases and seeing the same onstage presentations. Women frequently talked about how "humbling" various experiences and awards were. Winning was "humbling," different service projects they'd done were "humbling," waking up realizing they had "the honor" of "walking on the Miss North Carolina stage" was "humbling." I eventually picked up on it too, and soon enough was posting on social media about all of the "humbling" experiences I was having, especially having come from very "humble" beginnings.

I saw plenty of onstage quirks. When women were introduced onstage or were leaving the stage, they'd wave, but not in the way you'd wave to a friend across the room, elbow bent, shaking your hand from side to side. They only ever waved with their arm fully extended upward, hand precisely oscillating. Jewelry was never too big or too sparkly onstage. In swimsuit, nearly everyone wore giant five- or six-inch platform shoes from Chinese Laundry called "Tippy Tops" or a similar style. Many women took the well-known posed photo lying in bed pretending to sleep in their newly-won crown and sash. In onstage questions and in winners' post-win speeches, women frequently mentioned "bringing the Miss America crown back to North Carolina."

There was a collective desire to win the ultimate prize—the national title, Miss America—which had only been won by a North Carolina titleholder once since its inception. The less talked about goal for Black women wasn't just being the second Miss NC to win Miss America; it was being the second Black woman to win Miss North Carolina. When I was competing, only one Black woman had ever won in North Carolina—Deneen

Graham in 1983, the same year Vanessa Williams became the first Black Miss America.[*]

The quirks and peculiarities that made pageants unique also made them a breeding ground for prejudice. There weren't enough Black women competing. There weren't enough Black women advancing to the finals, and there was a frustrating prevalence of the token Black girl in the top five year after year without a Black winner. But the real problem was that our blackness itself wasn't welcome. The cultural and physical traits of Black women had no place in the system.

When I was competing in the Miss America system, I never once saw a woman of color in North Carolina win any local with her natural curls, an afro, braids, or dreads. If you were competing and wanted to do well, you knew to flat iron, perm, or relax and barrel-curl your hair or get a wig or extensions. Every contestant was required to have a platform we advocated for during the year, and you didn't see certain platforms promoted because they weren't considered relatable enough and were too close to blackness—such as destroying school-to-prison pipelines, fighting for more minority representation in leadership, or fighting for criminal justice reform.

African American Vernacular English? Not in pageantry. Not if you wanted to win. Speaking any way besides the English taught in schoolbooks, with the King James Version of a Bible quote interjected occasionally for flavor? Unacceptable. The way to critique a contestant who didn't fit the carefully curated mold that too often aligned with whiteness was to say that she needed more "polish."

---

[*] Alex Badgett became the second Black Miss North Carolina in 2019, several years after my competition eligibility for Miss North Carolina had ended and the same year the trifecta of Black women at the national level reigned.

It wasn't any one person feeding this environment. It wasn't any one individual's responsibility or fault. It was all of us. The blame rested with the people who advised that we conform, people who stood idly by while women erased their own cultural norms and uniqueness, and pageant judges who refused to advance nonconformers.

Any person of color understands this. We lack adequate representation in most professional industries. At one point in time when I was a law student, I was the only Black person on my school's moot court board of fifty-two students. I was the only Black woman in my entire full-time MBA class of fifty-three. I spent a fair amount of time as the sole Black lawyer in my law firm of nearly ninety attorneys. When I first began competing in the Miss America Organization in 2014, it would've been naïve to think that pageants would be excluded from this unfortunate trend in a country that, at the time, still had great difficulty admitting and reconciling its wrongs as they relate to race.

That is part of what made my win five years later so monumental.

• • •

Three and a half years before I stood in that hallowed chamber, I was preparing to crown the next woman who would hold my local title, Miss Metrolina. I gave each of the contestants my phone number and told them to contact me if they needed any help. I knew what it was like to be a newbie, to feel like I was on the outside of some secret society. I hoped to be a bridge to that society for the new contestants. A few women reached out, but one had a palpable, distinct hunger. Her name was Nia Franklin.

Nia was the kind of person who would reach out to me for advice, put my words to work, and come back and ask, "What's next?" She'd competed in a pageant for her undergrad university before but had never competed in the Miss America Organization and wanted some help. Coincidentally, she was enrolled in a master's program at the North Carolina School of the Arts in Winston-Salem, the same city I lived in while I attended Wake Forest. I gave her all the advice she wanted and was secretly rooting for her as the day of the pageant approached.

The night before the pageant, the contestants rehearsed their talent pieces to ensure there weren't any sound or technical issues. I was sitting in the audience, watching the nervous contestants practice, when Nia confidently walked onstage. Opera music began to play, and a heavenly, flawless voice sounded in the auditorium.

I leaned over to one of the committee members and asked, "Is she going to have a chance to sing without the voiceover playing?"

He chuckled before looking at me with enthusiasm and saying, "That's her voice."

I was floored. Nia sounded like she could walk into Carnegie Hall and fill up the room without a microphone. Her voice had a warmth, fullness, and control that made you sit and listen. At the time, the talent competition was the heaviest-weighted portion of the pageant. I couldn't wait to place a crown on Nia's head the next day.

Unfortunately, and to my utter shock, I never got that chance.

Nia did win a talent award the following night, but she didn't win either of the two crowns we awarded. I was happy for the women who won that night, but certainly wanted the diligent girl with the slam dunk talent to take the win.

Perturbed, but hopeful that Nia's pageant journey wouldn't end at this local competition, I shot her a message less than an hour after the pageant. I don't remember the exact words of the message, but I'm sure it was something along the lines of, "Don't you dare stop here." She didn't.

We became fast friends. Nia's outgoing personality balanced out my more introverted tendencies. And I was happy to continue helping her as her journey in pageantry advanced. She entered another local pageant, and I was there in the audience cheering her on while she lost another pageant she deserved to win. Afterward, she meandered off stage and met me in the audience section of the auditorium.

As we began talking, I could see tears welling up in her eyes, and I grabbed her hand and led her to the bathroom. I shared with her one of the unfair, unspoken rules you learn in pageants.

"You can't cry. You don't have the privilege of being honest about your disappointment or sadness or anger after you lose, and worse yet, as a person of color, we haven't had the privilege historically of showing anything but strength and joy. We don't have the privilege of showing anger or disappointment without consequences. And in pageants, you only get to ugly cry if you win."

Fortunately, I got to find out that Nia doesn't ugly cry when she wins. She was stunning in every photo of her being crowned on her third try for the local title that stamped her ticket to the state competition.

We turned our respective losses into big wins on two different national stages years later, but also turned them into a lasting friendship that benefitted both of us in many ways.

• • •

Nia, the reigning Miss America; my mentee Kaliegh Garris, the reigning Miss Teen USA; and I, the reigning Miss USA, strutted down the runway during our entrance for the RuPaul talk show. We were there to speak about our historic wins, the challenges we'd overcome to earn our respective titles, and why our wins mattered.

I was ecstatic that the three of us were doing so much press together. I had done individual phone interviews for a *New York Times* article about our wins beginning the day I touched down in New York City, and we'd begun doing press as a group since the second day of my media tour. *CBS This Morning* expressed interest in a sit-down with Gayle King and her cohosts. Sure enough, the Tuesday after my win, I was excitedly posing for photos with Nia and Kaliegh in the green room when Gayle strode in and introduced herself.

This meeting with Gayle took place just a couple of months after her earth-shattering interview with disgraced R&B singer and now convicted sexual predator R. Kelly. Gayle was a force to be reckoned with, taller than I'd imagined, and oozed a kind, warm confidence.

"How are you all doing?" she asked brightly.

"Great!" "Excited!" "Glad to be here!" we replied, all at once.

"I want to make sure I have your names right. Is it Chess-lee?"

"Kryst. Yep! That's it." It was a rarity for anyone to get my name right on the first try, but it wasn't a surprise that the ever-prepared Ms. King would.

After a minute of small talk, Gayle's team ushered her back to her desk before they returned from commercial break, and a producer walked in to finish prepping us for our segment. The three of us were elated to be on such a well-known news program, but more importantly, one that prominently featured a powerful

Black woman interviewing us about the power of Black women in pageantry.

The *New York Times* and *CBS This Morning* weren't the only outlets that wanted to cover us. This was the first time that Miss America, Miss USA, and Miss Teen USA were all women of color the same year, and people took notice. The three of us shot a spread for *O Magazine* together, we were featured in an article on the pages of *Marie Claire* magazine, and we had an iconic digital cover and spread for *Essence* magazine that ended up being one of my favorite photoshoots ever.

For the *Essence* cover, it was jaw-dropping to walk into a studio and see racks of clothing, two wardrobe stylists, three makeup artists, three hairstylists, a photographer, editors, and countless other assistants, managers, and content creators who were there just for us. The moment was made even more real to physically see the number of people who wanted to spread news of the moment we were having. Better yet, it was profound to see that nearly all of the people filling this room were Black. The makeup artists would know how to accurately match makeup to our skin, the hairstylists would understand how to do our hair, and the photographers felt and truly understood the photoshoot and the weight of this occasion.

When the *Essence* cover was released, it made a statement— it showed us with our crowns sitting on top of our natural hair that fell gently against latte, mocha, and chocolate faces.

"This is America," the cover headline proclaimed.

And in the reality and revelry, people still existed who did not understand the significance of our achievements and couldn't wrap their minds around why we were "still talking about race."

"Will Miss America's Outstanding Teen 2019 (a young white woman) be joining any interviews or appearances?" one

Instagram user commented on a photo of Nia, Kaliegh, and I from our RuPaul talk show appearance.

"I'm wondering this as well," another user followed up. "Doesn't speak well to inclusion and women's empowerment to not extend her an invite."

It was irritating to see that people were so accustomed to being included that featuring a small group of the historically excluded, placing us on more equal footing, made others squeak. I typically tried to ignore these comments but figured if I removed any wisecracks from my response, I'd be okay.

"Hey!" I started. "You might not have had a chance to listen to the interview we did on the RuPaul show and on CBS. The news story these outlets reported was about the three of us being women of color, so the outlets invited us—the three women of color—to talk."

The original commenter replied, "I love the fact that we have so many amazing women of color representing our nation." I truly wish she would've stopped there. It would've reflected at least an attempt to break out of her tunnel vision and realize that you can celebrate Black women alone, by ourselves, for the achievement we made alone, by ourselves, without including a white person who was not a part of the achievement or conversation. Alas, she continued.

"I do believe though that by only inviting three of the four women, it disregards the idea of inclusion and representation for all. Regardless, I love what y'all do. Keep on slaying the game."

I tried to explain what I could in the limited space allotted for Instagram comments: "I think the purpose of us being on the shows was to highlight the fact that women of color finally feel more included and represented, and it made sense to have just the three of us on to discuss this historic moment in time.

Not to oversimplify this topic, but, for example, if the story was about three titleholders being concert pianists, it would make sense for the news outlet to invite the three pianists. If the fourth titleholder was a dancer and not a pianist, she probably wouldn't appear on the show. Dancing is a great talent, but that's not what the story was about."

I understood the woman's point, I just vehemently disagreed with it. Her argument sounded like those who question why we still celebrate Black History Month. Or the white people who demand admission into or dissolution of historically Black colleges and universities, appalled that colleges could be built with the focus of serving Black people and ignorant to the bloody and bruised history that forced them to be built. They shriek about segregation and lack of diversity without knowing that HBCUs exist because white people denied Black people access to higher education. They forget that Black History Month was created because Black history isn't always taught in the same schoolbooks where stories about white people are written. In short, we were excluded, so we built our own haven. And now the excluder demands inclusion.

To bring equality to those without it, we must elevate those we've subjugated. Elevating others can look and feel like inequality if you aren't receiving the same elevation. But if you weren't browbeaten, tormented, lynched, and silenced, you don't need lifting; therefore, providing help solely to those who need it isn't inequality. It's equity. It's reparations.

The ironic part of the situation was that, by all accounts, Miss America's Outstanding Teen understood and supported the coverage Nia was getting for the important moment she was a part of. She seemed to comprehend that sometimes sisterhood means supporting your sisters while the spotlight on them grows, even if you aren't standing in its brightness with them.

The big question for far too many people was, Why were we still talking about race? Why did it matter?

Far too often, Black women in particular suffer from internalized tokenism. Exceptional Black women who ended up in C-suites and boardrooms, on courtroom benches, and as movie leads learned that there can only be one of us. That's often all that people made room for. Not only did it feel like extra pressure on our shoulders to be the best, it sometimes created a competitive environment instead of an uplifting one. We knew there was only space for one of us, and everyone else knew it too.

This one-spot-only reality played out in pageants in a number of ways. You didn't typically see more than one or two Black women in a top five at a pageant. And if a Black woman won, you knew you wouldn't see another Black winner for years. When Deshauna Barber crowned Kára McCullough Miss USA in 2017, having back-to-back Black queens was still an uncommon anomaly. And when Kaliegh won Miss Teen USA mere days before finals night for Miss USA, I felt joy for her well-deserved win, along with a brief feeling of doubt that I could win. What judging panel would crown another woman of color with natural curls right after Miss Teen won as a woman of color with natural curls?

My judging panel would.

My win helped quell my own internalized tokenism, and I knew I wasn't alone in feeling that way. Therefore, it was essential to talk about and celebrate our collective wins. Our crownings showed that Black has different shades, hair lengths, body types, ideas, interests, and accomplishments. Our wins demonstrated that more than one of us belong in a room, and more than one of us at a time can have a seat at the table, even when that means we have every seat at the table—all three.

We had no way of knowing that our three would soon increase to five and create an international moment.

• • •

My media tour and appearance schedule pressed on, past the interview on *CBS This Morning*, the Tom Brady flag football game, and the RuPaul talk show, to my homecoming. Each titleholder had the option of a homecoming, where she'd work with her state directors to organize events in her home state, celebrating her win. I wanted to make stops in a few different cities in North Carolina that were important to me—Charlotte, because it was my home; High Point, because year after year it hosted the state pageant I won; and Raleigh, because it was the state capital and the location of the law firm where I worked.

The highlight of my trip to Raleigh came when I was given the opportunity to sit down with a trailblazer: Chief Justice Cheri Beasley, the first Black woman to serve as the chief justice of the North Carolina Supreme Court and only the fourth Black woman in United States history to serve as a head judge of any state supreme court. As we toured her chambers and court-room, I noticed some portraits lining the walls around the room. They were large, detailed individual paintings of what looked like judges.

"Who are these people?" I asked.

"Those are the chief justices. Every person who served as a chief justice has a portrait hanging in this room," she answered.

"So, you'll have one too?"

"Yes, I believe mine will be on that wall over there." She pointed toward an area in the courtroom where the portraits began to look more recent.

I paused to think how powerful I would feel as an attorney, walking in to argue at the highest court in the state and seeing a portrait on the wall of someone who looked like me.

Chapter 6

LEARNING FROM MY LOSSES

"You learn more from losing than you do from winning."
I once said this in an interview, and it sounded good. Over time, life taught me to believe it.

In the midst of my homecoming and media week (which spiraled into months of media and interviews instead of seven days), I was still doing countless events as Miss USA. I announced the winner of the World's Strongest Man Competition in Florida on national television and did my official Miss USA photoshoot. I flew to Las Vegas to announce an award at the NHL Honors with Cat, after doing a skit onstage recreating the 2015 Miss Universe crowning mishap—host Kenan Thompson played Steve Harvey— and delivered opening remarks for the Big Brothers Big Sisters of America National Conference. I even went to Los Angeles to film a couple of episodes of a show called *Nashville Squares*, and while there I got to meet comedian Loni Love and former Miss USA Kenya Moore. We were featured on the show as celebrity guests, and then Kenya and I competed as contestants, pitting a former titleholder against the current one.

I'd heard Kenya's name many times before meeting her because of her role on the hit television show *Real Housewives of Atlanta*. My mom was a big fan of the show, and I'd seen clips of it over the years, including a memorable exchange Kenya had with one of her costars after she was erroneously introduced at a dinner event as a former "Miss America" instead of a former "Miss USA."

Confusing the titles was a common mistake that, even in my brief few months as Miss USA, I'd experienced myself. I learned I had a few different options to pick from when deciding how to respond. I could wait until people finished their sentence and subtly reintroduce myself, saying, "Thank you for that warm introduction and hello everyone! I'm Cheslie Kryst, Miss USA 2019." I could immediately interrupt the introduction with the correction, "It's Miss USA," and then allow them to finish. Or I could ignore the error altogether.

This was a careful balancing act, because I wanted to be introduced correctly with the title I'd worked hard to earn. I also wanted to be respectful of the Miss America Organization since those titleholders earned their titles just like I did, and I didn't want to be accused of posing as a Miss America when I wasn't one. But I also didn't like to embarrass people who either mixed up the titles in the moment because of nerves or didn't adequately research my correct title. Mixing up the titles was the equivalent of introducing the CEO of Nike as the CEO of Adidas.

Kenya later explained that she felt disrespected being invited to an event where the person introducing her didn't know her title, so she opted for correcting the host in the moment. Some people have criticized her actions, quick to pass judgment based on her heavily edited, pot-stirring reality series. The Kenya Moore I met was one of the most welcoming, kind, sharp, and gracious former titleholders I've ever known. When I met her in a production meeting at the *Nashville Squares* venue, she had an unmistakable presence about her that filled the room. Kenya was taller than I expected, as gorgeous in person as she is in photos, and she wore a skintight teal dress that showed off her hourglass figure. It didn't take her long to introduce herself to me and congratulate me on my win as Miss USA.

Kenya spent the rest of our time on the show asking how I was doing and pulling me into conversations with new people she'd introduce me to. She kindly gave me her phone number so we could stay in touch. We took photos together, and she was cheerful throughout the day, even after I won our head-to-head round in the competition.

As clichéd as it might sound, the sisterhood of Miss USAs was one of the benefits of the title. Being able to ask for advice or insight or receiving a kind word from a woman who had walked in my shoes was powerful, especially as I navigated appearances and press and started my preparation for the Miss Universe competition. Although no date had been announced, the Miss Universe Competition was inevitable. I was certain I'd have at least a couple of months' notice about the date when it was finally set, and I wanted to be more prepared for it than I had been for any other competition in my life.

I'd competed in plenty of pageants by the time I arrived on the Miss USA stage, and I'd lost more than I'd won. The prospect of losing another competition is what motivated me to work so hard on my preparation for the national pageant, where you only get one shot at the crown. Out of the fourteen pageants I'd been in before Miss USA, I won only six. The eight losses I notched are a large part of the reason I get to enjoy my successes today, and I learned to be thankful for each one.

My losses taught me some of my most profound and memorable lessons. Working hard and winning the first time around only motivated me to figure out the least amount of effort I could give the next time to produce the same results. In contrast, losing drove me to push the limits of possibility for myself, physically and mentally, and forced me to learn patience (sort of), discipline, purpose, and focus, all of which helped me later in life, on and especially off the pageant stage.

• • •

Most people know that attorneys must pass the bar exam—a long, difficult test—to practice law. Far fewer people know that, in addition to the bar exam, another test is required in all but two US jurisdictions: the Multistate Professional Responsibility Examination. According to my law school colleagues, the MPRE was supposed to be a straightforward, easy test. At least compared to the bar exam, which measures a person's knowledge of standards of professional conduct. But nobody should've told me it would be easy.

I studied for a couple of nights in a row before the test, assuming most of the exam would be relatively intuitive. Turns out it wasn't—at least not for me. This multiple-choice exam required you to know things like, are attorneys required to report alleged misuse of funds being held in trust for a client to a disciplinary authority, and if so, should they report it because they are required to report all violations of professional conduct, or should they report it because the issue raises a substantial question regarding the attorney's honesty, trustworthiness, and integrity as a legal professional?

I didn't know.

And I failed the exam.

Actually, you can't fail, per se. You just don't earn enough points on the test to meet the required score in your state, which makes you feel like a failure anyway, so it's basically the same thing. The scary part of failing the MPRE wasn't that I couldn't retake it. It is administered three times a year, so I could easily retake it in time to start the job that was waiting for me post-graduation. The horrifying part of failing the MPRE was knowing that I didn't pass the easy test, and the hard test, the bar exam, was just over the horizon.

Failing the easy test turned out to be quite fortuitous for me, because it was just the motivation I needed to stress-study for ten weeks during the summer I prepared for the North Carolina bar examination. Call it "Scared Straight" for this future attorney. I asked my best friend to change all the passwords on my social media accounts so I couldn't log in. I turned off news notifications on my phone so I wouldn't get distracted or end up going down a rabbit trail after seeing a salacious headline. I told my family, who lived only an hour and a half away from me, that I wouldn't be home to visit at all during the summer. "Please don't even invite me," I typed into our family group text. "I'm not coming." That meant missing Fourth of July cookouts, family movie nights, and any sense of normalcy.

I built a routine of arriving on campus by 9:00 a.m. to sit in a room with my study partner and watch our bar exam course. Then we'd eat lunch and study some more, and I'd go home around 5:00 or 6:00 p.m. to watch a movie before heading to bed. The only reason I refused to study after I left campus for the day was because my brain worked quicker and could digest information more efficiently the next day if I committed to a reliable clock-out time and some rest. The choice was entirely strategic. If not for those undeniable benefits, I would've studied late into the night, every night.

My self-care activities consisted only of getting my nails done during my lunch break every couple of weeks (I eventually had them all cut down to nubs before the exam so I could type my essays faster), going to the gym (no more than an hour at most, to conserve time for more studying), and occasionally browsing online for a new apartment. Not a single day went by without me thinking about, counting down for, or crying over the impending bar exam.

It worked. I passed the North Carolina bar exam on my first attempt. At that point, I had never worked so hard for something in my life. I had never prepped for any one competition for that length of time, studied for a class that diligently, or used that much willpower for anything I'd ever done. A failure at my back, and the prospect of deep embarrassment and uncertainty about my job in front of me if I didn't pass, summoned a level of focus and discipline I knew I possessed but hadn't called upon before. Failure and fear ended up teaching me a great deal. Yet that wasn't the only lesson I'd learned from failure.

Before law school, I ran track and field in undergrad for the University of South Carolina, and my last meet was unforgettable in the worst way. The Southeastern Conference is one of the most competitive in the country for many sports, including track and field. Placing in the top eight in an event at the SEC meet—the only placements that earn points for your team—typically meant you were one of the best athletes in the entire country. The woman who scored eighth place in long jump at the outdoor SEC meet the year I graduated from South Carolina leapt 19 feet 11.75 inches. The lowest placing All-American women's long jumper at nationals the same year jumped 19 feet 9.5 inches—meaning that you had to jump farther to score a single point at the conference meet than you did to earn All-American placement at nationals.

During my senior year, the conference track meet happened to be scheduled the same weekend as my college graduation. I convinced my coach to let me stay in town for my graduation ceremony in South Carolina, then leave an hour after the ceremony to fly to the University of Missouri for the meet, where I'd compete in the long jump the next day. The travel itinerary was meticulously planned, and since my graduation was in the afternoon and I had a connecting flight to catch before landing late at night and competing the following afternoon, I didn't have room for anything to go wrong.

So, of course, something went wrong.

My chaperone for the trip and I made it out of the Columbia, South Carolina, airport on time and landed at Dulles airport near Washington, DC, on schedule. Unfortunately, a pretty bad storm descended after we landed, and our flight was delayed. Tons of other flights had been grounded as well, and everyone had somewhere they needed to go. A feeling of urgency and panic swept the waiting areas as the storm raged outside, lightning occasionally igniting the dark sky looming on the other side of the large airport windows. Gate attendants sprinkled across the terminal hurriedly shouting announcements to the throngs of people surrounding each desk.

During the commotion, my chaperone and I missed our connecting flight that had been rushed out when there was a brief break in the storm. The next flight wasn't scheduled until the following morning.

After the anxious night, our flight got us to the competition in barely enough time for me to shower, put on my uniform, and arrive at the meet. The guy I was dating at the time—a professional track and field athlete and Olympian—was at the venue. He told me I looked tired when I sprinted down the runway to the long jump pit. The comment stung a bit coming from him, but he was right. I was distracted and tired, exhausted both physically and mentally. Most detrimentally, I kept complaining to myself in my head about how exhausted I was, which further convinced me that I wasn't going to do well.

And I was right. I didn't place, didn't earn a single point. That season, I hadn't jumped a distance that was ranked highly enough to advance me to the regional competition that was scheduled after the conference meet; therefore, I couldn't advance to nationals. My track and field career was over. Rather than going out with a bang, it meekly fizzled.

My failure at the conference meet didn't hurt too badly at the time. I'd already been accepted to law school at Wake Forest University and was looking forward to a summer without having to worry about staying in shape or doing intense workouts in the Columbia heat. I'd never planned on going pro and so, even though I would have liked to advance, in the grand scheme of things, it didn't realistically matter whether I ever made it to nationals.

Much later, I realized the real lesson that emerged from my experience as an athlete. The lesson was one of regret. I got to law school, met new friends, and swapped stories about my undergraduate years. My career as an athlete was an easy response to the common first-day-of-school "tell us a fun fact about you" query. The follow-up questions were the real challenge. Yes, I had been a Division I athlete, but no, not an All-American. I was top ten in the record books at South Carolina in the triple jump, but never scored at the conference meet. I won a second-place medal at the Penn Relays in the triple jump, but never made it to nationals. Recovering from stress fractures in my spine and other injuries early in my collegiate career weren't impressive success stories of overcoming, because my athletic career didn't have a fairy-tale ending.

My performances told the story of an above-average athlete, but not an elite one. Accepting that reality was difficult because, looking back, I realized I could have done more. I hadn't fully committed to being an athlete in any way. I could have improved in plenty of areas. I could have dedicated myself to a healthy diet, been more committed during training, focused on my mental game, and been more cognizant of how I took care of my body during recovery periods. I wish I could look back at my journey with pride, knowing I gave 100 percent of myself to the endeavor, but I didn't. And the slow realization that I sold myself short has nagged at me ever since.

If I could turn back time and start anew my freshman year, I'd walk out onto the worn red Mondo track on an eighty-seven-degree September day for my first track and field practice, feel the heat radiate from the ground up past my ankles, line up next to that mix of All-Americans, national champions, and collegiate record holders, and do everything differently. I wish I'd had the same focus then that later helped me pass the North Carolina bar exam and later the South Carolina bar exam in one attempt each. Feeling the unrelenting regret of my track experience— and knowing I never wanted to taste it again—informed some important decisions that paid off years later.

Studying for two different bar exams taught me how far I could push my personal limitations. The most powerful lesson I learned was that when you meet fear, you have to thrust yourself into it rather than retreat from it.

My worst subject when I was studying for the North Carolina bar was real property. Even though I scored in the 90th and 97th percentile for three subjects in our proctored practice exam, I scored in the 37th percentile for real property. I didn't care an inkling about countless concepts in real property like deeds, land sale contracts, wills, easements, fixtures. The mere mention of some of these terms made me drowsy.

Working on the topic was uncomfortable. And doing mini practice tests on the subject was scary, especially having to review multiple choice questions and one by one mark my answers wrong. Sometimes after I finished a practice test, I had to take a few minutes to talk myself up before I could work up the nerve to review the answers.

But I knew it had to get done. And even when I was afraid of how poorly I performed, the only way I was going to improve enough to pass the big test was to trudge through my fear, panic, and discomfort day after day. That's the same way I approached my prep for Miss USA. It's what helped me win. And it's how I planned to approach my preparation for Miss Universe.

After I became Miss North Carolina USA and set my sights on the Miss USA competition, I used every waking moment of time in the day for preparation—at least, every moment when I wasn't working full-time as an attorney, running a fashion blog, and doing speeches, volunteer work, and appearances. I was exhausted. Every day. There was no guarantee I would win the national competition, so in my mind, I needed to prepare as much as I could without igniting the ire of my law firm. Before I won my state title, I hadn't even told them I was competing.

Inspired by my bar prep methods, the approach I used for my Miss USA preparation was unforgivingly brutal. I woke up every single weekday at 4:45 a.m. I'd flop out of bed—literally, some days, falling to the floor beside my clanging alarm clock—stumble over to my closet, pull some athletic clothes on, and brush my teeth before running in the dark to my car.

Still, I was routinely the last arrival at my 5:10 a.m. cycle class at the local YMCA. Yet I always made it just before the workout started. After class, I'd rush home, shovel some breakfast into my mouth while reading a newsletter so I could keep up with the top US and international stories, then shower and head to work right around 7:00 a.m.

My day would usually include a mix of working at my desk and traveling, driving or taking the train to hearings at our Raleigh office. I'd also fit in appearances when I could. Some days I'd leave for a long lunch break and drive to a local venue for a speech before heading back to the office and staying a couple of extra hours to make up the time I'd missed. My ten-year-old SUV was on its last leg for most of my reign, the dashboard constantly blinking annoyingly friendly indicator bulbs like the engine light or check oil light. When I had to drive more than thirty minutes for a hearing or an appearance, I'd borrow one of my siblings' cars or my mom's vehicle the night before or walk a few blocks from my downtown office to a rental car shop, where I could snag a tiny sedan for two days for about sixty dollars.

After work, or on my lunch break when I wasn't booked, I'd talk to one of the numerous interview coaches I worked with. The closer I got to leaving for Miss USA, the more we talked, and in the months leading up to the national competition, we went over mock interview and onstage questions twice a week. On weekends, I'd catch up on work projects and blog articles that had fallen through the cracks during the week.

This routine was exhausting and taxing on my body, my energy, and my mental state, but I'd been there before. It wasn't much worse than shutting down my life to study for the bar for up to ten hours each day. And, like I did when I was taking the bar, I isolated my weak areas and worked on them. Swimsuit and evening gown were straightforward and fun, but I dreaded the interview and onstage questions.

I used to read commentary from pageant fans who would point to me being a law student, and then a lawyer, and reason that I must be great with the interview. Not the case. The first few interviews I did in the Miss America system were awful. I heard comments suggesting I was too serious and brought no personality or warmth to the interview room. Stereotypical lawyer problems. And that was in the Miss America system, which is known for intentionally making interviewees feel like they're the White House press secretary fielding questions from a room of bloodthirsty reporters. The Miss Universe system seemed to want someone who could answer political questions, yet be warm, kind, and personable. I had a lot of work to do.

Instead of ignoring the problem and caving in to my fear, I turned back to what I'd learned from studying for the bar: I would find my weak points and attack them.

I challenged myself to pile daily mock onstage questions on top of my already-full schedule and force myself to finish in thirty seconds each. I was already doing mock onstage question practice with my interview coaches, but I could squeeze in three hundred more questions if I did my own solo daily practice. Online, I found a list with hundreds of mock onstage and interview questions, a mix of tough political and social issue questions and easier, softball "What does beauty mean to you?" questions.

Each morning after I finished my shower, I'd stand in my bathrobe and stare into my bathroom mirror, pull five slips of paper one by one out of the baggie of questions I'd made, and answer them aloud, timing myself with my phone. I started adding a few to my evening regimen as well, looking online for onstage questions from past Miss USA and Miss America competitions. After finding videos of the question portions, I'd listen to the host ask the question, pause the video, answer the question while timing myself, then play the video back to compare my answer to that of the contestant.

Beyond my daily onstage question practice, I began to think deeply about my views on various topics I thought I might be asked about. I kept a journal with notes from my coaching sessions, a list of my goals, and other random musings. Soon, I carved out a section in the notebook solely for hot-button, widely discussed issues and my thoughts on them. Abortion. Gun control. Climate change. Marijuana legalization. Suicide. Race relations. Transgender rights. I wrote these down in my notebook and left a few blank lines under each topic.

Routinely, I'd flip through that section in my notebook, touch my pen to a topic, and think about or talk through my perspective on the issue. If it was a topic I didn't talk about often, I'd add a one-liner that summed up my thoughts or a punchy statement that would be impactful. *Trans rights are human rights. Immigrants are not the problem—violence is. The answer to gun violence is not more guns.*

I worked myself to the bone. I prepared for every scenario, question, or surprise change I could think of. The only part I didn't prepare for was losing. I simply refused to carry that visual in my mind. I'd dreamed about winning my state title before I won, and leading up to the Miss USA competition, I dreamed of winning that title too. That's all I was focused on: learning from my losses and leaving no stone unturned while I prepared to win.

Even though I did everything in my power to make sure I'd perform well at Miss USA and planned to do the same as I inched closer to Miss Universe, my many years of competing taught me that anything can happen at a pageant. You don't know what happens in the interview room, you don't know what the director has told the judges about what they're looking for, and you don't know how the judges perceive what happens onstage. I've left competitions singing the praises of the results and walked away from other competitions dumbfounded by what had transpired. I've seen state and national titleholders lose at small local competitions shortly before winning big later on.

The subjectivity inherent in pageants makes them confusing and exciting at the same time. Pageants are not like track and field meets, where you look at a time or a distance and the best is undeniable. Pageants are more like arguing with someone about whether Michael Jordan or Serena Williams is the greatest athlete of all time. Or whether Justice Ruth Bader Ginsberg or Vice President Kamala Harris is more influential. Influential to whom? And for what? And when? One contestant may seem more personable and authentic, but a more seasoned competitor could come across as more confident when answering her onstage question.

The key to winning is being prepared in every category—and hoping for the best.

Chapter 7

A PUZZLE I COULDN'T SOLVE

Although everything in my public life was on an upward trajectory, my personal life was in shambles. Despite my best efforts, which included taking time off from my once-in-a-lifetime job and devoting the majority of my free time to my boyfriend, my relationship was collapsing in front of my eyes.

It hurt to go to appearances with my mind clouded by our issues and arguments. It hurt to get up in the morning knowing the fun and joy would be sucked out of the day. Even worse, it hurt to realize the problems were nothing new for us, despite what had felt like a storybook start.

Justin and I first met in high school. I was a freshman on the cheerleading team at a rival high school, and although he was a sophomore on the opposing school's basketball team, he approached me and asked for my number. We didn't date, but we stayed in touch. Eventually, we attended the same high school and undergrad university, and we lived in the same town while I was in law school. When I was about to graduate with my law degree and MBA, he asked how I was celebrating. I invited him to my graduation dinner with some family and friends and to one of my graduation ceremonies.

What I liked the most about his presence at the graduation dinner was how well he fit into my circle. Going to the same schools and living in the same communities meant he knew many of my friends and had hung out with one of my brothers. Beyond that, he had a charm that made people feel like they were his friend, even if they'd just met him. That charisma drew me to him after I graduated, in spite of my decision to spend some time as a single woman.

I'd made the decision during law school to stay away from relationships, after I discovered a damaging pattern I'd fallen into. The role social media played in society grew substantially between 2012 and 2017—when I was finishing undergrad and going through law and business school—especially via Instagram and Twitter. These platforms made it easier to have an audience I would've otherwise had to somehow meet in person. I used to have to go to a party or bar or event to have a guy ask for my number. Now I could post a thirst trap and expect a few private messages or new follows. I had countless options, a roster of eligible bachelors at my fingertips, so many that I could end a relationship one night and be out to dinner with another guy the next.

For a while, this habit worked well. I never had to sit in sadness from one lost relationship for long because I could mask it with the joy, excitement, and intrigue of my next relationship. I had options and I used them, never having to be alone, and successfully avoiding the true magnitude of sadness after I stopped dating someone I genuinely liked.

The process was robotic and inauthentic. I realized I was dating placeholders rather than people. I couldn't always answer the same questions I'd ask the men I dated. What *did* I do for fun? What kind of music *did* I like? Did I play this music because the guys I liked happened to enjoy it and I wanted to curry favor with them, or was I listening to it because it moved me?

By the start of my fourth and final year of law and grad school, I'd moved into a new apartment and was living alone for the first time in my life. I'd left most of the organizations I'd joined in law school and business school, resigning from leadership positions or not running for new ones. And I'd stopped going out to parties or daytime social activities as much. I was tired of doing things just because they sounded good, other people were doing them, or because I thought I was expected to do them. I needed to discover my own passions. What kind of person was I? What did I like to do in my free time? (When there was such a thing in my schedule.)

I hadn't answered these questions for myself when I graduated from law school and moved to Charlotte to start my work as an attorney at a midsize firm, so I knew I wanted to stay single. I wasn't opposed to casually dating but didn't want to jump into a serious relationship.

"We need to talk about why I don't want to date anyone right now." "That's one of the reasons I talked to you about not wanting to date anyone right now." I'd had this conversation with Justin before. "I think it's hard for people to understand my schedule, but I love my brand-new, big-girl job. I love working hard, and I look forward to going to work. It's what I've spent my entire life preparing to do, and now it's finally here. I don't want to compromise my work because I'm focusing on a relationship, and I don't want to drag anyone's feelings through dealing with my schedule and not being able to see me and constantly wondering what I'm doing."

I was honest. I *didn't* want to be in a relationship. I didn't want to have to be accountable to anyone, least of all a man. I had a vision for myself, and it didn't involve rushing home to see a boyfriend. It was essential for me not to make a relationship (or a search for one) my life's focus or to measure my self-worth based on a relationship status, both of which I'd done before and wanted to break free of.

Plus, Justin wasn't the only guy I was seeing at the time. I split my weekends between seeing him and seeing someone else I'd recently begun flirting with, and I loved it. I felt like Olivia Pope with Mr. President/Justin on one end and B613 operative Jake/handsome, chiseled Malakai on the other end.

Justin was the person I looked forward to talking to at the end of a long day; Malakai was the person I wanted to stare at. He worked out every day, and you could tell. While hiking together on a hot day one weekend, he took his shirt off, revealing a rippling six-pack, thick pecs, broad arms, solid shoulders, and a defined back that I'd seen in photos on his social media but not in person. I tried not to openly gawk at him, so I sat down on some rocks behind him, opened my phone camera, and gazed at him through the screen while I pretended to send a text message to a friend.

I thoroughly enjoyed spending time with both of them. It felt like the best of both worlds.

Things were going well for a couple of months, until Malakai posted a photo of the view from my apartment balcony on his Instagram story. A guy friend of mine who knew both Justin and Malakai mentioned it to me.

"I saw that photo Malakai posted," he said, smirking a bit.

"What photo?" I asked.

"You know . . ." he replied, side-eyeing me. "You have a pretty unique balcony."

ABOVE: Cheslie
as a student at
Huntingtown Farms
Elementary School

LEFT: Cheslie
as a Fort Mill
High School
cheerleader

ABOVE: Cheslie and April on a school field trip to the North Carolina Governor's Mansion

RIGHT: Young Cheslie was an equestrian who loved horses

ABOVE: April crowned Mrs. North Carolina US 2002, standing between Mrs. Tennessee and Mrs. United States 2001, Dana Opsincs

LEFT: Promotional photo of April as Mrs. North Carolina US 2002, posing with her crown and sash

ABOVE: April in her mint-green, two-piece ball gown in a white horse-drawn carriage

RIGHT: Cheslie crowned Miss Fort Mill High School 2009

ABOVE: Cheslie's
University of
South Carolina
graduation
photo, 2013

LEFT: Cheslie
doing the triple
jump for the
USC team
at a track &
field meet

Cheslie competing in
the long jump for the
USC track & field team

Crowning Cheslie as
Miss Metrolina 2015

ABOVE: Cheslie at her MBA graduation from Wake Forest University, May 2017

LEFT: Cheslie being recognized by her fellow law school graduates as the only person in their class to receive the dual degrees of MBA and JD (Juris Doctor)

Cheslie playing the piano during the Miss North Carolina pageant in 2015

Cheslie in the tuxedo she wore during the talent portion of a local Miss North Carolina pageant

Cheslie and Kate Peacock as the top
two for Miss North Carolina 2015

Cheslie after
she was
crowned
Miss North
Carolina
USA in 2018

TOP: Cheslie in her "Black Lawyers Matter" hoodie

BOTTOM: Cheslie and Victoria Paul

TOP: Cheslie and Victoria posing in black at rehearsal

BOTTOM: Cheslie and Victoria running backstage at the Miss USA pageant

Cheslie on stage
after being crowned
Miss USA 2019

With T-Pain after
she was crowned

Photo courtesy of Miss Universe Organization

TOP: Posing with the pageant hosts, Nick and Vanessa Lachey

BOTTOM: Cheslie being escorted by security into the winner's suite

TOP: Watching the big-screen TV in the winner's suite

BOTTOM: Catriona "Cat" Gray (Miss Universe 2018) and Cheslie in New York

Cheslie and
Nia Franklin
out hiking

Cheslie and Nia at Miss America 2020

Cheslie visiting with Cheri
Beasley, the first Black woman
to serve as Chief Justice of the
North Carolina Supreme Court

Trifecta of Black queens, left to right: Nia Franklin, Kaliegh Garris, Cheslie Kryst

He wasn't wrong. My apartment was in a popular area in Charlotte called South End, and my balcony was on the top floor of an apartment complex that overlooked a line of bars and sat next to the unmistakable light rail train that led to the downtown area. It didn't help that I'd posted the view on my own social media platforms countless times.

"So . . . ?" I said, trying to play clueless.

"And weren't you just hiking around the same time as a friend of ours?"

Sure enough, both Malakai and I had posted hiking photos around the same time from the same area of Crowders Mountain. It wasn't intentional, and I didn't think anyone was paying attention enough to put two and two together. I hadn't lied to either Malakai or Justin about each other, but I'd spent enough time with both of them to know their feelings would be hurt if they knew about one another. It was time to pick one guy.

One day, I was mulling over this decision while at a café with my brother Asa. He and I both went to South Carolina for undergrad and were only a couple of years apart, so he knew both Malakai and Justin. I told him about my dilemma, and he agreed that I should consider focusing on one of them before things got dramatic or stressful.

"Well, who do I pick? I like both of them," I told him.

He paused, thinking before answering.

"Justin! Everyone likes Justin."

He was right. Justin always had a gaggle of friends around him wherever he went. He knew my family, and people he hadn't met instantly liked him soon after being introduced to him. He was never in a rush to leave when we were hanging out with a group of my friends instead of his. To seal the deal, my brothers preferred him, and on top of that, he was one of my favorite people to talk to. I always looked forward to calling him after work, even if we'd been texting all day. We were spending more and more time together, and he was the only person I could see myself giving up my rosy year and a half of singledom for. So, I did.

Justin and I soon became exclusive. Initially, it was blissful. We spent nearly every waking moment talking to each other, texting each other, or hanging out together. It was about four months in when I began to sense a change and grew suspicious.

There was nothing big that I could complain about. Instead, a thousand little things bothered me, and beginning to bring each one up made me feel crazy. Justin lived four and a half hours away, and even though I used to command most of his time while he was home, things had completely flipped. Now it seemed like every time he came to town, his friends were the first ones he saw. He'd arrive in the late afternoon after work on Friday and hang out with them until the early evening. If he didn't go out to a bar or club with them, he'd come and stay the night at my place. On Saturday, he would golf and hang out with his friends all day, head to a bar that night, and then spend most of Sunday hungover, sleeping on the floor at my house until he recovered enough to drive home.

He was also more distant in our conversations than usual. He stopped resharing stories I'd post on Instagram of the two of us together. Occasionally, he'd overshare information that I'd normally have to ask about a couple of times. Once, he called me from his brother's house in Charlotte and told me he'd been talking on the phone with his ex-girlfriend. No problem, I knew they shared mutual friends. She was a former pageant titleholder herself who had told me to keep competing: "We need more of us out here." We followed each other on Instagram, and I had nothing but admiration and respect for her and her accomplishments in the pageant space.

He said he felt obligated to talk to her because she was going through a hard time, and I said I understood completely. Later, though, he told me she was begging him to take her back, after she'd experienced an especially difficult breakup with her boyfriend. It was hard to believe until I listened to a recording he had of her crying on the phone to him about how perfect they were together when they dated. But all the extra details and tidbits of information he shared with me still seemed out of place.

Every now and then, I'd ask him about some of these strange pieces of what seemed like a giant puzzle I couldn't solve. These conversations always ended in an argument. He told me he couldn't understand why I didn't trust him, since he'd done nothing to betray my trust. I couldn't point to any one incident that countered his reasoning, and I began to wonder if I was losing my mind. One night, I decided to get to the bottom of it. I'd look through his phone. If there wasn't anything suspicious or unsavory in it, I'd drop the issue.

• • •

It was midsummer in 2018, and Justin came to my house late on a Sunday night, after a full day of hanging out with his friends. Again. I would have liked to have at least shared a meal with him, but instead I'd spent most of the day writing articles for my fashion blog and doing some studying for the South Carolina bar examination. I'd passed the North Carolina bar the year before, and, since my firm's Charlotte office had a fair number of clients in South Carolina, it made sense for me to take the South Carolina bar as well.

Justin was tired and fell asleep quickly when he arrived at my apartment, but I was wide awake. Adrenaline was surging through my veins, and my hands were slightly shaking while I waited in the darkness, listening as Justin's breathing grow louder and slower. I whispered his name a few times to make sure he was asleep before I leaned over and pulled his phone from the nightstand beside him, replacing it with my phone face down in case he woke up.

I turned over to my side of the bed, slid the covers over my hands and face, and unlocked his phone, relieved he hadn't changed the password since the last time he'd shared it with me. I typed his ex's name into the search bar in his text messages and, seeing nothing, swiped through his call log. When I didn't see a single call between the two of them, I began to worry. He'd already told me he'd been talking to his ex on the phone. Why did it appear that he'd deleted all the evidence?

Next, I found a group chat with his closest Charlotte guy friends and scrolled through it, discovering a message that made my body feel numb. Justin and I had talked about his birthday, which was about a month away, and he'd told me he wanted to celebrate with me and his friends on a boat ride. He and his friends were talking about it in the chat.

Yeah, but Cheslie will be there, so I won't be able to be up on any hoes.

He wouldn't be able to what?

I was deeply hurt. I knew my suspicions and fears were right, and my gut feeling wasn't steering me wrong. I also knew that the more I looked, the worse it would get, but I wanted to see it to be sure. Instead of continuing to scroll through his phone beside his sleeping body and risk discovery,

I slowly slid out of bed, tiptoed to the other side of my apart-ment, flipped on the light in my guest bathroom, and locked myself inside.

Sure enough, the more I peeled through his text messages and his Instagram DMs, the more disappointed I grew. I suspected that he'd deleted a fair amount of his misdeeds, but I saw enough evidence to show me that his gaslighting and denials were covering up a man who thought he could do whatever he wanted. In one private message on social media, a woman asked if he was dating anyone, and he told her he was "talking" to someone but not in a relationship. That was almost three months after we'd decided to become official.

Another girl DMed him her number. And one unsaved phone number texted him after what appeared to be a very drunk night of his, saying something to the tune of, "Hey, this is Amber, if you remember me from the bar last night."

I placed his phone in front of me on the floor and sat there for a moment, processing what I'd seen and putting together a plan of action. The crushing pain I felt because of the betrayal I'd read was softened by relief that I wasn't inventing problems in our relationship. Instead, my Spidey-senses had been detecting inconsistencies from a liar. I wasn't crazy. I was right.

Taking a deep breath, I unlocked the door and coolly walked back to my room, in disbelief at the audacity of this man sleeping so peacefully in my bed. Didn't he know that I knew? I flipped the light on and nudged him awake. He took a while to rouse and was still a bit confused as he opened his eyes. It was about 2:00 a.m.

"Get dressed," I told him, somehow maintaining a calm but insistent tone.

In his bewildered, half-asleep state, he sat up and began pulling on his pants, eyes barely open.

"Quickly, quickly, quickly," I said, composed and firm, laughing a little in my head while I watched him fumble for his shirt.

It only took a few more seconds of blindly following my instructions for him to finish waking up. He looked at me, red-eyed, and said, "What's going on?"

"You have to go," I responded. "Now." It brought me a sliver of joy in the moment watching his confusion, but I also didn't know what emotional response I'd have if I had to tell him what I'd found. I'd maintained my composure to that point but wasn't sure how much longer it would last.

"Cheslie, what's happening? Why do I have to leave?" he asked, peering up at me while he sat on the bed half-dressed. I almost felt sorry for him but also wanted to throw a glass of water in his face. I paused, taking another deep breath before I told him.

"I looked through your phone. I saw all of it. And now you have to leave."

"Saw what, Cheslie? What are you talking about?" he pleaded, still attempting to maintain his innocence.

"Everything." I walked toward the front door, with him closely following behind. "You know exactly what you did. I trusted you, and now we're done." I grabbed his keys on the way to the front of my apartment and pushed the door open.

"Goodbye," I said firmly, handing him his keys after he slid his feet into his shoes.

"Cheslie! It's the middle of the night. I don't know what you're talking ab—"

"Leave," I said loudly. My voice echoed in the hallway outside of my door.

He walked through the doorway and turned around to say something I didn't catch as I slammed the door shut. I hurried back to my room to make sure he hadn't forgotten anything. Rolling my eyes when I saw his watch on the nightstand, I reached for it just as I heard a knock at the door. Perfect timing.

I snatched the watch from the nightstand and marched to the front door as the knocking continued. I yanked it open and, as I suspected, Justin was still there. I dropped his watch in his hands as he looked at me, pleading. "Please, Cheslie, I don't know what you're talking about." I didn't respond as I closed the door again, locked the deadbolt, and flipped the light off. I waited a moment and looked through the peephole to see him staring at the door before turning on his heels and trudging toward the parking garage.

I walked back to my bed and straightened the sheets where he'd nearly dragged them off while dressing in his stupor. I slept soundly that night. My relationship was in the toilet, but I was vindicated.

* * *

Toxic relationships never begin that way. At least not in my experience. They begin beautifully. Flowers. Attention. Time. Kindness. They devolve into ugliness and gaslighting. People wonder why women stay in these relationships. They ask us why we never left, which is the wrong question. The right question would be: Why do men in these relationships commit to toxicity? Why doesn't society demand they do better? To complicate things, even without these inquiries, it is hard to leave when you've seen the relationship at its incredible peak, when you were a team. You sincerely believe you and your partner can get back to that. For me, I was convinced the relationship was over because of the chipping away at that belief and seeing that the worst it was at any moment was the best it was ever going to be again.

After I booted Justin from my apartment, I began to regret not screenshotting any of the evidence I'd found. He texted me the next morning, apologizing for his behavior and the way he'd talked about me. "I really don't have another way to explain it other than me and my friends talking is just me and my friends talking, being guys of course. I talk a big game and speak freely with these guys."

The gaslighting continued. "I know you're upset, but I seriously hope you don't want to throw away our relationship. Please give me the opportunity to talk through this."

I wish I could say I resisted his sweet-talking. I did at first. I texted him back and told him I thought we should take a break. At this stage in his life, he needed some more time to be single. But he insisted he'd just been too friendly and was putting on an act for his friends. That much I believed—he was putting on an act.

Insecurity can sometimes parade as arrogance. Secure men don't have to prove to their friends that they can "get girls" or "pull hoes." Men who carry deep self-doubt feel like they have to talk about and demonstrate their prowess. I was staring a common case of toxic masculinity in the face. I fell victim to its consequences because my boyfriend wanted to show off to people who cared more about him being the source of their amusement than they did about how their misguided expectations would wreak havoc on his romantic life.

In a way, Justin and his friends were victims of toxic masculinity too. When music and movies and friends and role models repeat the same thing to you over and over again—honoring and revering emotional unavailability, praising lack of vulnerability, sexualizing and objectifying women, and mocking monogamy— it's difficult to break free and cling to your own set of values and principles.

I wondered whether Justin was a bad person or if his poor choices were a result of poor influences. I thought deeply about the age-old nature versus nurture question: How much of who we are is who we're born as, and how much is a result of what the world impresses upon us? Was Justin capable of being faithful? Would he have been capable if he wasn't such a people person and a people pleaser? Was he someone who needed to earn loyalty and admiration from friends, even when it cost him love? And if I could show him what I thought was happening to him, could he change? Would he?

We talked later that night, and he told me he hadn't been able to sleep the night before—I refrained from pointing out that he'd had at least a few hours of sleep before I kicked him out—and he hadn't eaten or worked that day. I could tell he was upset and regretted what he had done, and his insistence that he hadn't done anything wrong made me wonder if I was overthinking the situation. Plus, even though I made it to work, I also hadn't been able to eat or get him off my mind the entire day either.

Although you may think I'm crazy, three things convinced me to stay with him. First, I'd never been in a relationship for longer than four months before dating Justin, and we'd just reached the six-month mark. I'd developed a pattern of leaving other relationships at the first instance of trouble because I didn't want to waste my time. I followed my instincts even when I feared I was being unreasonable. Every argument was cause enough to break up. This time, I made the conscious decision to do what I could to make my relationship with Justin last, because I wanted to see what it would look like if I resisted my urge to run. If I stayed and looked past some bumps in the road, maybe I'd find out how so many people I knew had made their relationships work.

The second factor that kept me with Justin was the impending South Carolina bar exam. I was days away from beginning my one-month sabbatical from work, and I knew the heartbreak from leaving Justin would make studying even more difficult than it already was.

Third, I thought he would change. That may sound naïve, especially in hindsight, but I'd seen him do better and at the time believed he could return to his better self.

I listened to all of Justin's promises to honor our relationship, and I stayed. Candidly, even today I can't honestly say whether it was the right decision. I did end up passing the South Carolina bar. As much as I hate to admit it, staying helped me to remain emotionally stable and focused enough during my weeks of studying leading up to the test. I needed that. I could keep my feelings in check for a few days, but it would've been hard to keep the tears away for weeks on end. By the time the bar was over, Justin and I seemed to be in a better place, so there was no reason to break up with him right after I passed.

But then, Justin cheated on me not even four months later, making out with some girl the night before I won Miss North Carolina USA. I found out the morning of the competition, a mere three hours before I walked into the interview room with the judges. I held it together the rest of the day because I refused to let another one of this man's indiscretions keep me from my dream. Studying for the bar twice gave me an elite ability to compartmentalize my feelings for brief time spans when I needed to.

I arrived back in town after the competition, drove to his house, and dumped in his driveway the few belongings, gifts, and photos he'd left at my apartment. My pain and anger convinced me that I should have broken up with him when I first saw the deceit and lies his ego drove him to tell. But when those feelings waned, I wondered how that choice would have played out and whether I would have known if it was the right decision.

Chapter 8

DISTINGUISHING MYSELF FROM THE COMPETITION

As my year pressed on, I began to feel the fatigue of constant travel and lack of routine. When I was an attorney and our interns would ask what practicing law was like, I'd say, "What I love about it is that every day is different! I may be at my desk all day working on pleadings or doing research or I may be at another office doing mediation or I might be in court arguing a motion. You never know!"

When I was practicing, almost every event in my day fit within a nine-to-five-ish window. Sure, there was travel here or there and some nighttime after-hours events or fundraisers, but for the most part, my morning and evening routine was the same. As Miss USA, I wasn't always sure what state I was in or time zone of the country I woke up in. I didn't know if I'd be doing an interview that would air on VH1, leading a chant in front of a football stadium with over seventy thousand people looking at me, or flying to Brazil to work with one of the pageant organization's nonprofit partners. Once, I was in four different states in less than twenty-four hours.

Oftentimes, I didn't know what time I needed to wake up the next morning until I received my schedule at the end of the day. It didn't seem difficult to handle at first, but I didn't anticipate the many small changes. For example, it was challenging to schedule lunch with friends, plan a doctor's visit, or set nail appointments. I learned to keep my phone on a charger as much as I could or keep a portable charger at the ready, in case I had a last-minute event or my day ended up going longer than I had projected. I figured out workouts that I could do in my room in case the hotel I was staying in didn't have a gym.

At first, I hesitated to ask for time off, for fear of appearing ungrateful or looking like I wasn't dedicated to my role. You only get to be Miss USA once, so I figured I could stick it out for a year or however long it lasted. But I soon understood I wouldn't enjoy my reign as much if I was constantly worn out and exhausted. Plus, my memory suffered when I was endlessly on the go. Speaking engagements were more difficult to do well, particularly without notes.

I talked with Esther, MUO's director of talent, about it, and she started building a day or two of rest into my schedule when possible. In July, she kept my calendar clear over the Independence Day weekend, so I could go home and take a trip to Charleston with my boyfriend and his friends. I was grateful for the time away, even though I was still supposed to dress up one of the days and do some media with a Charlotte news outlet. I'd just wrapped up two separate West Coast trips and had a patriotic-themed photoshoot with BET that was due to drop on the Fourth. I posted the photos and article from the shoot, along with some pictures and video on my Instagram stories of fireworks down in South Carolina, while I enjoyed a few concurrent days of relaxation for the first time since before I'd won Miss USA.

Justin and I hadn't been doing well, so I made sure to request a couple of days away to celebrate his birthday. Unfortunately, while I thought I was adding to my personal life, for some, this was perceived as taking away from my professional life.

I'd worked with countless people leading up to Miss USA, but there were four coaches I spoke to more than once. Bill Alverson was one, a fellow attorney who'd coached women for decades. Another, Heather Sumlin, I spoke to nearly every other day leading up to the competition, and she coached me on interview and onstage questions more than any of my other coaches combined.

The other two coaches were a pair of former Miss USA titleholders who had coached me privately a handful of times over the years and whose workshops I'd attended as well. I liked that they were former titleholders, because they seemed to have an inside look at what worked well at the national competition. They'd coached two recent Miss USA winners, and though I didn't talk to them nearly as often as I worked with Heather, they had given me helpful advice about branding and how to stand out among the other fifty women at the competition. We'd decided the fact that I was the only practicing attorney in the group was important.

One of my coaches told me that, to the extent it made sense, if I made it to the onstage question round at Miss USA, I needed to start my answer with, "As an attorney . . . " It was a subtle way of continuing to distinguish myself from my competition and remind the judges of who I was and what I'd accomplished. Sure enough, when I received a question about the #MeToo and #TimesUp movements, I worked the "as an attorney" phrase into my answer, and the audience erupted into applause. I was grateful for all of the help and guidance I'd received from each of my coaches.

Sometime after my win, the coach who'd advised me to lean into my uniqueness as an attorney appeared on a podcast, and I tuned in to hear what she had to say. I wasn't surprised when the podcast began with a message explaining that she'd coached me and two other recent Miss USA winners.

The podcast episode was about whether pageants were still relevant, a fair question. When Miss USA and Miss America were first being broadcast on television decades ago, they pulled in tens of millions of viewers. Over the years, ratings for both pageants had slipped significantly from their heyday. The year I won Miss USA marked the first time in years that ratings hadn't dropped from the previous year, and even then, the broadcast pulled in three million viewers, which was third place in the ratings for the night. In my view, this decline happened for a number of reasons.

First, when pageants began, TV was simpler. There were fewer channels. Three major networks—NBC, CBS, and ABC—provided most of the programming. Streaming services, increased competition, and the ability to record programs has eaten away at viewership for all television, not solely for the Miss USA telecast.

Beyond simple viewership, pageants have faced an identity crisis in the United States in recent years. Formerly, pageants didn't have to highlight the substance of each titleholder as much as they do now. They could position themselves as the governing body for defining beauty and give you a pretty titleholder who could stand and wave and smile and take photos and preach world peace occasionally, similar to Sandra Bullock's character in the movie *Miss Congeniality*. To my dismay, that seemed to be what my former coach was advocating for in the podcast—specifically, for a return to the era of the Miss USA pageant's former owner, Donald Trump.

"Love him or hate him, he was great at pageantry because this is a man who loves beauty and beautiful things and, I mean, I've been in his apartment, and everything is coated in gold. I don't know if they sell, like, gold paint at Home Depot . . . " she said.

"I think he probably had it melted down and physically, like, put on his wall," the male host responded.

"Probably!" my former coach laughed. She talked about the previous glamour and excitement of being Miss USA, when she was a titleholder in the early 2000s. She talked about going to P. Diddy's annual White Party in the Hamptons and "brushing the shoulders" of celebrities and meeting the princess of Thailand.

"What you just pointed out, everything comes down to one thing that I think Trump did really well, and IMG is not doing very well—and that is marketing," the host said. "Miss USA was very visible. You know, when you were Miss USA, you know people literally found you on the street and were like, 'Wait a minute, you're Miss USA!' Now, I don't know if Cheslie gets that. I mean, I haven't talked to her about it, but I kind of doubt it. I mean, you don't see her on the front pages of magazines that are outside the pageant world. You don't see her on the cover of Page Six, or doing huge interviews, or hanging out with celebrities."

I felt betrayed. Angry. This was a guy my family had welcomed into the winner's suite with us to celebrate with my close friends the night I won Miss USA. He'd texted me encouraging words and notes leading up to nationals, and now it felt like he was delegitimizing my existence. With one of my coaches! Sure, most of their criticism was directed at the organization and it seemed like I was just collateral damage, but if they were willing to speak about me like this on a podcast, I couldn't imagine what they would say about me behind closed doors.

Sadly, I wasn't the only one caught in their crosshairs. The former titleholder mentioned me and two other clients she'd worked with by name and, in short, said we didn't seem busy enough and maybe we didn't "seem as relevant to the world."

"Those three ladies pretty much all have had a lot of downtime, where they're able to take a weeklong vacation and go see family and they're able to spend time with their boyfriends and it shocks us. Why do you have all this downtime?" she said.

My mental health was hanging by a thread, my relationship was sifting through my fingers like sand, and my old coach was making me feel like I was doing a terrible job as she managed to talk about me behind my back and to the public at the same damn time.

The worst part of it was that the podcast host specifically introduced his guest as my coach at the beginning of the call, which, in my view, made it seem like I condoned or agreed with what they were saying. I didn't.

It seemed the kind of "celebrity" they wanted Miss USA to be was exactly the kind that led me to compete in the Miss America Organization before the Miss USA brand focus shifted from beauty to highlighting the depth and breadth of the accomplishments and personalities of the women who competed. I didn't think less of the women who enjoyed the competition the way it was before or simply acquiesced to the requirements in order to get a chance at the opportunities the title provided. I simply didn't feel like I could justify to my law firm my competing in a pageant that seemed to focus more on beauty than substance.

Two things kept me in good spirits and helped me refrain from any real dramatics. First, even though it felt like everyone in the country had heard about the podcast, only people in the pageant community listened to or heard about it. Second, their assessment was off, to say the least. I *was* recognized on the street as Miss USA; I wasn't being hounded like Beyoncé would be, but even today I'm appreciative and flattered when people occasionally stop me and ask for a photo. I was doing huge interviews: *Inside Edition, Good Morning America, CBS This Morning*, Yahoo News, E! News, Now This News, SiriusXM, BET, VH1, AOL BUILD, *Marie Claire, O Magazine*, and countless others covered me during my media week and throughout my reign.

I wasn't on the cover of Page Six, mostly because it isn't a standalone print publication. Back in the day, it was literally *the sixth page* of the *New York Post*, which was where the gossip section of the publication was printed, and the *New York Post* had indeed covered my reign: first running an article about my win, then an exclusive on my Miss Universe costume and the meaning behind it, after the podcast had been released and again to celebrate the "groundbreaking Black dynasty shaking up the pageant world" that I happened to be a part of. That was the kind of coverage I wanted. Inspiring. Full of purpose.

I also knew the digital cover of *Essence* that I'd already shot with Nia and Kaliegh was supposed to be released the next month, I was due to walk the red carpet and appear in a segment onstage for BET's Black Girls Rock event, and an episode of a show I'd filmed for the Oprah Winfrey Network was due to air in the next few weeks. Even better, earlier in the month I'd interviewed for and earned a job as a correspondent for a major entertainment news program and was scheduled to do my first couple of interviews in a few days, with actress Millie Bobby Brown and singer Lizzo. Rather than reaching out to my former coach or the podcast host, I decided to be patient and wait for them to find out for themselves.

Despite my disappointment in their statements, I understood what they were saying. They wanted Miss USA to be a bona fide celebrity, like Rihanna or the Kardashians. But the truth is, in the last two or three decades, becoming Miss USA doesn't make you an instant celebrity anymore. It opens doors and gives you connections, but the Miss USAs who are legitimately famous became that because they leveraged the opportunities the title provides. My former coach was and is a prominent fixture in the pageant community, but her self-described "celebrity status" extended only to a few episodes on a popular reality TV show and a handful of gigs in the entertainment industry.

Of course, some women who competed in pageants did become famous. Gal Gadot, Halle Berry, Vanessa Lachey, and Olivia Culpo all competed in the Miss Universe system, as Miss Israel, Miss Ohio USA (and first runner-up to Miss USA 1986), Miss Teen USA, and Miss Universe, respectively. However, their fame and success did not come solely from competing—otherwise, year after year countless Oscar-winning, blockbuster moviemaking, international models would be lauding pageantry as a springboard to fame. In a time when women can get famous from growing their following on social media or appearing on popular reality television shows, there isn't as great a demand for pageantry as there once was.

The celebrity space nowadays is noisy, cramped, and competitive, and although it's a little easier to push into that space with a crown on your head, growing your own success and maintaining it is a challenge. This is especially difficult when some dedicated pageant fans don't want the reputation of pageantry to change. Some want beauty and glamour to continue to reign supreme in the pageant space and don't like the changes the organization has made to ensure judges and audiences hear more about the women, their backgrounds, their goals, their opinions, and the incredible things they're doing in their communities. They don't always want the parts of pageantry that require shattering the mold of the tall, slender pageant girl with blown-out hair and a kind smile. They're resistant to the parts of the pageant that add substance, which would leave us with sparkly gowns on statuesque bodies, two-piece swimsuits clutching bouncing breasts and booties (and I'm not talking about shoes), and a quick but meaningless interview and onstage question round designed only to ensure contestants can string together a comprehendible sentence—the stereotype of pageantry that too many people still believe in.

The problem with this reputation in modern society is that people today don't want a titties-and-ass show if it is designed only for the male gaze and only celebrates one kind of beauty, but doesn't have a message or purpose tied to it. We want sex-positive empowerment, not sexualization for profit. Miss USA and most other pageants are *not* T&A shows. But Miss USA still has a swimsuit portion, which prompts questions from some news outlets about whether pageants objectify women. The existence of the swimsuit portion of the competition is enough to trigger discussion about the sexualization of women and commodifying women's bodies with no benefit to the women themselves. On one hand, in the height of the #MeToo movement, the Miss America Organization seemed to respond to some of this criticism by eliminating its swimsuit competition. On the other hand, Miss USA kept the swimsuit portion, and although the organization has made incredible progress, it hasn't completed the transformation the overall competition needs to convince occasional viewers that it is not objectifying.

Coincidentally, the discussion of the swimsuit portion—whether it is objectifying and the ways various organizations react to it—is largely representative of the broader discussion of whether pageants as a whole are objectifying and why. An excellent example of two contrasting paths to take when it comes to matters of beauty and women's bodies is the success of the Savage X Fenty lingerie show versus the now-defunct Victoria's Secret show.

In recent years, Savage X Fenty has presented a highly-produced and entertaining show that features women of various shades, races, body types, sizes, ages, and backgrounds. Professional models, dancers, drag queens, and celebrities entertained on-screen among a mix of performances from rappers and singers. The lingerie was colorful and made for all types of women, and men were added to the show too! The styling, makeup, and hair were edgy and provocative, and the show was positioned as one that would represent and celebrate all: truly inclusive. Rather than broadcasting the show on network television, the colorful affair was delivered on a popular streaming service.

Conversely, before going belly-up, the Victoria's Secret show faced criticism from people who argued that the show was anything but inclusive, displaying decadent and expensive lingerie that wasn't available in a wide enough range of sizes or shades. The show itself featured a constant barrage of tall, slender, mostly white women, and the year before its final show, an exec was quoted as saying they weren't casting plus-size or transgender women in the show because it was supposed to be a "fantasy."

The two brands are the definition of inclusivity versus the good ole boys club. The female gaze versus the male gaze. Representation versus inaccessibility. Sex-positive versus sexually objectifying. The problem with Victoria's Secret's "fantasy" approach (which it appears to have now abandoned, since it appointed Megan Rapinoe, Priyanka Chopra Jonas, Paloma Elsesser, and others in 2021 to help reframe its brand) was that today, lingerie is not just an item men buy for the women they want to have sex with. It is something we women are buying for ourselves, because we like it, and we want to look and feel good in it. Therefore, you can't effectively market a garment when women see it on an hourglass figure with minimal body fat and think, *That will look incredible on her and only her. I can't pull that off.* You need women to think, *She looks like me. I want to buy what she's wearing because it looks incredible on her and will look incredible on me too.* That's part of the challenge of pageantry today. Many pageant fans want Miss USA to be a Victoria's Secret Angel, when the world has demonstrated a preference for the Savage X Fenty superstars. We have to build a show and a brand that people can relate to. That they can see themselves in.

Although I'm not privy to the higher-level discussions of strategy for Miss USA or the Miss Universe Organization, it seems like they've been working to take the Savage X Fenty route, welcoming a transgender contestant at both Miss Universe and Miss USA recently, celebrating their part in the Black queen dynasty, and adding capes and sass to the swimsuit competition, but it's taking time to finish the transformation and convince potential new audiences that we've changed. I wanted to do that during my reign and did my best to share the message in interviews about what's changed in the organization. I highlighted the substance the competition worked to show to viewers, including contestants' accomplishments beyond the pageant arena and the tremendous impact the women were having in their communities.

It has taken a while to understand that some pageant fans want to evolve with the times, and some don't like change. Maybe we'll eventually lose those rigid few, but the silver lining in any loss is the lesson you take from it—even when the loss is the end of friendships. Eventually, the podcast host apologized to me about his comments, saying he understood why I thought they were insensitive.

My former coach also became my former friend. I never sought her advice or coaching again. After the podcast aired, I solely worked with her business partner, and the only times I talked to her were to extend a couple of cordialities when the need arose. I wanted to be able to seek her advice as I started my Miss Universe preparation, but I didn't feel like I could trust her. I felt like we both fielded a loss, but I was glad to take away a lesson from it. As you grow and change, your life will show you different sides of your friends. Some will stay on the journey with you. And some won't.

Chapter 9

THE SLOW BURN OF SOLITUDE

Although Justin and I had resolved to just be friends, we soon entered a toxic cycle of making up and breaking up—even if I suspected he was lying about something, we'd get back together after he cried and pleaded and negotiated his way back in, or after I came running back to him.

The happy parts of that cycle were a mountainous peak of joy and sacrifice. Justin found a job in Charlotte and moved back to the city for the first time in years. He spent holidays with my family. He took me on vacations, bought me gifts, and scheduled couple's counseling sessions. His drinking slowed down, and he was going to bars less often. He rarely missed one of my calls or FaceTimes. And he started asking me if I was okay with him going out with his friends or traveling, which felt like a mix of him asking for permission and wondering if it would hurt my feelings or bother me if he went out. I never said no; I just wanted him to be honest with me about where he was going and who was with him.

Unfortunately, our relationship's high points didn't shield us from the dungeon that our lows created. I thought that if Justin changed, our relationship would survive, but though he was changing in some ways, he was doing it out of obligation to me, not out of a genuine desire to be a good partner. Honesty was a constant issue for him and was one of the reasons our relationship felt like it was nearing its final end. When I found out about his infidelity, he initially denied it and swore on his deceased mother that he hadn't cheated on me. Days later, he admitted that he'd shared "two pecks" with a girl while I was away competing.

By the summer of 2019, we'd done a couple of sessions with the counselor Justin had found. In one of them, I told our counselor I felt like a prison warden rather than a girlfriend, tracking him and feeling in the pit of my stomach that he wasn't telling me the truth. The counselor looked Justin square in the face during our session and said, "Do not lie, ever."

Justin froze. I felt validated. It was the first time someone who had nothing to gain and hadn't claimed a side made me feel reassured, like I wasn't crazy. I'd spent so much time doubting myself and apologizing for my valid emotions that it was a relief having someone say that demanding honesty, even for the little things, was a reasonable expectation. This truth is part of what gave me the conviction and the nerve to leave for good.

In August, Justin and I had a few bad weekends in succession. He never hit me, but I began to fear for my safety. We had an argument, and he flew into an alcohol-fueled rage, punching through a large glass frame I'd gifted him, which held a photo collage of us. There was broken glass and blood everywhere. More gaslighting, more lying, and more tears followed, due to apologies and a temporary resolution. I was supposed to stay with him the night it happened, but I slept in a car instead, too embarrassed to go home to my mom's house and alert her to what was happening, and too cheap to get a hotel room in the middle of the night.

We were just days past this event when Justin was supposed to travel to Charleston for a friend's birthday. As had become his routine, he texted me to ask if I was okay with him going, driving down on a Thursday night and driving back to Charlotte on a Saturday.

"Of course!" I replied. "Have fun and tell everyone I said hello."

He'd be there with a group of couples I'd met before, the birthday bachelor, and a few others. I thought it odd that he wouldn't stay through Sunday to complete the weekend but didn't question it until Saturday. He texted me the morning he was supposed to be leaving and said that the birthday celebration was still going. There was going to be a pool party and dinner or a bar visit—or something that I wasn't listening to—as I prepared myself for what was next.

He asked me if I minded if he stayed another night.

"I won't be upset or anything. You're my number one priority," he wrote. "It's up to you, baby—whatever you want me to do. I just don't want to make any waves or upset you."

I'd never said no. Ever. I didn't need him to ask me for permission; I just wanted to know what the plan was. This time was different. I couldn't place my finger on it, but this change of plans felt strange.

"To be completely honest, I'd rather you not, but if you're asking, I think it's clear you want to go. So, go."

"You'd rather me not stay or go to the party? Do you want me to call you? Wanna talk about it? I just don't want to upset you," he answered.

"It's going to upset me. But I can't be the one to come between you and your friends. Go to the party, stay the night, since I know you'll be drinking. We can talk some other time."

"Lol nah," he texted, "I won't. Thanks for being up front this time though."

Just an hour later, he called me and tried in vain to convince me that he wasn't going to do anything wrong, that he was with a bunch of couples, not some guys going out to get girls, and that I should be fine with him staying.

"You asked if it would bother me. It will. It doesn't matter to me what the circumstances are—I've said what I said. I can't make you go home. You asked what I felt, and now it's your turn to make a decision about what you're going to do."

"What am I supposed to do if I drive back to Charlotte?" he asked. I was sitting in the titleholder apartment in New York City, so it wasn't like I would be there waiting for him when he returned. And it didn't sound like he was eager to catch an impromptu flight to see me.

"Visit your family. Hang out with the rest of your friends. Do your schoolwork." He was taking remote classes to earn his MBA.

He continued to try to reason and sway and persuade me, but I was firm. I was also irritated that he'd spent so much time over the previous months asking me if I'd be okay with him going out, only to still go out the one time I said I didn't feel comfortable with it. Why ask if it changes nothing?

He stayed in Charleston. And I was through. His decision was the teeny-tiny, itty-bitty, microscopic scrap of straw that broke the camel's tired old back. I'd planned to spend Saturday working on my fashion blog but was now consumed with our argument, my imagination running wild manufacturing reasons for his decision, my mind's eye flooded with nightmarish visuals of the trouble I believed he'd get himself into. Again.

I couldn't take it anymore. I'd broken up with him before, but it never stuck. We talked so often every day that it barely took twenty-four hours before I was back to calling him or he was back to pulling me in. I needed to do something that would make this time the last time. After a year and a half together, I broke up with him in a text message. Then, I texted my favorite ex-boyfriend. (Always the eager rebound. We'll call him X.)

I was scheduled to be in North Carolina for an appearance the following week and decided I would see X while I was there. I was tired of the constant stress and anxiety of my relationship with Justin, and I finally admitted to myself that things with Justin were never going to get better.

Justin and I stayed in contact, even though I'd broken up with him. An abrupt breakup wasn't easy. Ours was long, slow, and torturous. In one exchange, he asked me if I was talking to anyone, and I answered truthfully, telling him I was in contact with X. He demanded to see my phone so that he could read my messages, later telling his friends I was the one who'd cheated on him. I was furious.

"STOP TELLING PEOPLE I CHEATED ON YOU, I DID NOT," I wrote in a text message to him. "THAT'S MESSED UP TO LIE ON MY NAME. I will NEVER speak to you again."

I did, though. Yet eventually, as the sting of heartbreak numbed, I stopped talking to him altogether. What helped the most was my coming to the slow realization that *I was Miss USA, damn it.* I was single, living in New York City. I picked my head up from the sorrow that was my crumbled relationship and felt the bright, warm sun of singledom on my face, welcoming me to a new arena of freedom.

My year was picking up more steam than it had in the previous whirlwind months. I'd been offered a temporary position that was going to introduce me to plenty of new people, offer more opportunities for travel, and possibly give me a new career path. The timing was quite convenient. Fortuitous, even.

I dove fully into the single life, like a kid jumping into a pool on the first day of summer. I didn't want to be single and would've preferred being in relationship, but I wasn't going to continue to weather toxicity. I wanted to enjoy my reign, and if that meant singling and mingling, I was going to do it. There were countless beautiful restaurants in the city, and I had reached the point in my relationship with Esther where I felt comfortable telling her when I had a date and wanted to have the night off.

When I started removing photos of Justin and me from my social media platforms, the messages from suitors began to increase. I even went back to a couple of the DMs I'd received from celebrities the night I'd won the Miss USA title and started new conversations. I downloaded a few dating apps, including one someone had told me was a celebrity dating app. It was supposed to be like Bumble or Tinder but strictly for famous people. After sifting through my phone to find my favorite photos for my profile, I started swiping. Most of the people in my queue were in the entertainment industry, and I saw a few bona fide A-listers as well.

Via the dating apps, I soon discovered a plethora of guys in New York City at my disposal. Surgeons, high-powered attorneys, finance brokers, and entrepreneurs were interested in me. I went out with a comedian, a reality TV star, and an actor, and reconnected with a guy I'd had a crush on in law school who'd moved to New York after graduation. I even shot my shot at a famous crush I saw on the celebrity dating app. Thinking he wouldn't notice me on the app, I slid into his DMs and asked him out for coffee. It was the first, and only, time I reached out to a guy to ask him on a date. Zero for one, but I'd do it again if I knew I'd get a response.

I was picky about who I'd entertain beyond a couple of dates or phone calls, and I didn't want to get too serious with anyone. Living in the titleholder apartment was a welcome excuse I'd give for not inviting my flirty suitors home with me, and my unpredictable schedule was an excuse to not stay out too late and to turn down the occasional late-night sleepover invites.

As much fun as I was having, I felt like I was still recovering from my traumatizing relationship with Justin. It was years before I told my siblings many of the details, and there were some things I couldn't say out loud. After I told them, I was most worried about whose side my brothers would be on. One of my brothers had been friends with Justin for a long time, and I didn't expect him to suddenly end the friendship because of the things I was telling him, including events that had played out years before.

I wanted to get back to the old me. The me who liked being single, whether I was going out on dates or not. The me who loved my work, enjoyed my life, and didn't feel like I had to run home to talk to a guy or stress about what my partner was getting into in my absence. One of the most difficult parts of that adjustment was dealing with the stinging feeling of loneliness in the still moments at the end of each day.

My loneliness had little to do with physically being alone. I was rarely alone while I was traveling and speaking and doing interviews as Miss USA. It had more to do with periods of genuine connection. I could be surrounded by crowds of people in a massive room yet feel drained and lonesome. I hated the monotony of small talk about the weather, so even when I was having a conversation with a person, I didn't want to feel like someone was absently hearing me talk. I wanted to feel reached. I wanted to share space with someone who just got me. As an introvert, I didn't need that feeling constantly. I feel pure, clear, sunshiny joy when I'm alone. But that time is not infinite. It ends, and I need genuine connection again.

That is part of what made it so hard to finally leave Justin. Our relationship had become an addiction for me. I loved being single, but I grew to love talking to him more. Especially when he would step out of a meeting to take my call or get up from a dinner to FaceTime me. It was hard to stay away when I began to feel the slow burn of solitude, craving the sweetness of someone asking me how my day was because they truly wanted to know.

But sometimes loneliness is the cost of self-respect. I'd been on a payment plan for a long time, trading pieces of myself, small chunks of my dignity, in exchange for quality time and "good morning" texts. It was time to take my self-respect, dignity, and value back. And I did.

Chapter 10

TRUSTING MY INSTINCTS

Before long, my disappointment over the pageant podcast about MUO's missteps—and practically, by extension, my failure—had subsided somewhat. A major reason for that was because I already knew about a few plans in the works regarding some new opportunities for me, including a gig with *Extra*.

One day, I went into the MUO office to meet with Jackie, the director of PR, who asked me about my interest in a unique job.

"Have you ever thought about being an entertainment journalist?" she asked.

I hadn't. I didn't even know what the job of an entertainment journalist would entail. She listed a few names I recognized of people in the field and explained a little more about a new role she thought I might be interested in with *Extra*. A producer who'd covered the Miss Universe and Miss USA pageants over the years had reached out to Jackie and explained that *Extra* was looking for a New York correspondent. After seeing an interview I'd done and looking into my background, the producer sought me out for the position.

Although I didn't know much about what I was getting myself into, I was intrigued. I told Jackie I wanted to hear more and was interested in giving it a shot. Before long, I was walking into a meeting with one of the New York–based producers and listening to his description of the show and their plans for its newest season, which was set to begin in early September. This meant that our August 9 meeting was less about gauging my interest and more about vetting me for what would be my first and surest step away from the legal industry and the life I'd known before Miss USA.

As I listened and thought more about the producer's description of the work I'd be doing, I realized it was the perfect opportunity for me. I loved pop culture, followed celebrity and entertainment-related news, and often discussed and debated these types of issues with my friends. I'd always had a curious (okay, nosey) nature about me and loved burrowing down a rabbit hole into the background, motivation, and life stories of high-profile or infamous public figures. Despite the more serious tone and setting of the courtroom, I'd garnered plenty of experience in formulating and asking questions when I was an attorney conducting depositions. And before that, as a law student participating in trial competitions, I had learned about litigation and cross-examining witnesses.

I loved listening to people's stories and telling my own. But it was the back-and-forth arguments and need to think on your feet that alternately scared me and made my mouth water at the prospect of winning a battle of wits in the courtroom. I developed a taste for conducting interviews early in my time as a law student, and it looked like I was now going to be able to put that drive to practical use on TV.

I was on pins and needles after the *Extra* meeting, waiting to hear whether I'd be given a shot. Not long afterward, I was ecstatic to hear the producers wanted me to join the team as a special correspondent. My jaw dropped open upon hearing that they already had a few interviews lined up for me, with stars including Lizzo, Zendaya, and *Stranger Things* star Millie Bobby Brown.

Overcompensating in preparation for my first few gigs, I studied and watched hours of interviews that each of these women had done, thinking of questions I wanted to ask them and imagining how they would respond. I could see us laughing at one of my jokes; I envisioned them being captivated by the incisive questions I'd written; and I was convinced I was going to leave each interview best friends with each woman I was scheduled to meet. Looking back, my idealism makes me laugh.

As the time approached to meet with Millie Bobby Brown (MBB), I received an email with information for the date, time, and place of the interview, some background information on her, and a list of suggested interview questions. After asking a bit more about the ins and outs of the process, I learned that the *Extra* team that puts together the segment writes questions that fit the story they're trying to tell. The focus could be a bit about the unique fashion sense a celebrity is known for that leads into a newsworthy moment about a new clothing line they're releasing. Or the story might be about an awards show and the funny highlights from the night.

My interview with MBB was packaged into a segment about a new skincare line she was releasing, with a few mentions of *Stranger Things* and how shooting was going sprinkled in. I spent the morning memorizing my questions so I wouldn't have to look down at the notecard I had prepared. My preparation turned out to be more helpful than I could have imagined. When we started the interview, I discovered how often the plan for what questions I'd ask and in what order I'd ask them wasn't always going to pan out the way I intended. Knowing the full slate of questions helped me jump around a bit. The conversation was more organic, and we didn't have to return to subjects we'd already alluded to earlier, or miss an opportunity to dig deeper when I heard a surprising answer.

Next up was Lizzo, and I was thrilled that the *Extra* team had come up with an idea to use my crown as a prop during the interview. The idea was that Lizzo was an emerging music queen, and she deserved a crown. Coincidentally, I'd walked to one of her songs during the swimsuit competition at Miss USA.

The *Extra* team and I met at a hotel where Lizzo was holding court for a few different interviews in a row. Jackie and I trailed behind a producer; an audio tech lugging what looked like a bag full of wires, some microphones, and a square box with a bunch of dials on it; and a cameraman pulling a giant camera and other necessities. We walked into a hotel suite and were met by a couple of representatives from an alcohol brand that Lizzo had partnered with and a second group of people from a competing entertainment news show. I was already nervous, and now I was meeting my competition in a hot room that was feeling smaller by the moment.

Thankfully, even people who work for competing shows are collegial, friendly, and helpful. There's a sense of we're-all-in-this-together-ness that has developed over years of standing shoulder-to-shoulder at red carpets and occasionally shuffling producers, talent, and others among the stations. The producer on this interview greeted the team from the other show with a smile, and I followed suit. We all chatted for a bit while the cameramen and audio teams set up. Lizzo and her vivacious presence entered the room with a small team of people. At the time, she was the most well-known celebrity I'd ever been in a room with, and she was just as beautiful in person as she was on TV.

Jackie, the *Extra* team, and I shuffled into the bedroom of the suite while we waited for the other entertainment news team in the living room to talk to Lizzo first. I ran through the questions in my head a few more times before walking out, greeting Lizzo, and beginning our interview.

Aside from the beads of sweat I could feel forming on my nose and forehead, the interview was going well. Lizzo beamed with energy and personality once the interview started. She was still flying high from a smash-hit performance at the MTV Video Music Awards. Once I told her about our plan to crown her as a queen in her own right, she was absolutely on board. I filled her in on information about where my crown came from and whipped out the decades-old pearl-and-diamond treasure that was the Miss USA Mikimoto crown, valued at just under a quarter of a million dollars.

"I'm really proud of you!" she told me as she recalled the three history-making wins that had made Black girl magic a thing in the pageant world.

I held up the iconic bejeweled crown and told Lizzo to face the camera as I stepped closer to her and got ready to place a piece of history on her head. The crown itself is incredibly front-heavy, given its shape. An adjustable band, made of silver and shaped like an oval, forms the bottom of the crown, and diamond- and pearl-encrusted silver feathers are molded to the front of the band, leaving the sides and back of the band bare. If you place the feathers of the crown close to halfway between the front and back of a person's head, with the band circling around the natural crown of the head, the weight of the crown leans backward ever so slightly, and its weight is balanced by the silver band pressing into the back of the head. The crown also has a small comb attached to the inside front, which helps to catch and hold its weight once it's placed on the wearer's head.

When I placed the crown on Lizzo's head, I realized I had placed it too far forward. Lizzo, fully in character, was making her own version of the pageant-winning cry face and went from squatting slightly while I crowned her to standing and commanding her moment. As she stood, it was too late for me to lift and readjust the crown, so I held the back of the silver band, keeping the band from lifting up as the crown tipped forward.

As I navigated this literal balancing act, Lizzo was working the camera and brightly enjoying her crowning moment. She realized I was still partly holding on to the crown and playfully pushed me away so she could have her full alone time to shine. I stumbled backward a bit, releasing my hold on the silver band. Immediately, the Mikimoto crown tipped forward and fell off Lizzo's head. I felt like I was watching it in slow motion.

All I could think was, *This crown has years of history sitting on the heads of Miss USAs like Crystle Stewart and my fellow North Carolinians Kristen Dalton and Chelsea Cooley. It's survived traveling across the country and, out of all the different crowns various Miss USAs have worn in the title's seventy-year history, it was my favorite one. And now I'll be the Miss USA that goes down in history for breaking it.*

Everyone in the room saw the crown tip off the front of Lizzo's head, and we all collectively reached for it. Thankfully, her quick reflexes caught the silver band of the crown just as it descended toward her hips on its way to the floor. The laugh that followed from everyone in the room was obviously out of nervous relief mixed with joy.

● ● ●

As my interviews continued, I worked to sharpen my skills and be a sponge for feedback from my experienced and creative *Extra* colleagues. I took time to think about the questions I was given and mused about how I would respond or react to receiving them on the other side of the table. I'd had countless people interview me in my first months as Miss USA. I remembered interviewers who seemed well-prepared and genuinely interested. I also vividly remembered the ones who asked challenging questions that gave me pause.

One of those questions came during a long-form interview for an online series, with an experienced journalist who'd clearly done her research on me and on the topics she planned to discuss. Although most of my interviews were shorter than ten minutes, this one was supposed to last at least twice that amount of time. As we began, I immediately liked the interviewer and enjoyed the dialogue we had, which was sparked by thoughtful and informed questions. We talked about my thoughts on the swimsuit competition, statistics about the lack of representation for women and people of color in leadership in the worlds of business and law, and the success of the #MeToo movement. Even though I'd touched on each of these topics in other interviews, it wasn't often that I dove deep into these subjects or talked about all of them in the same sitting.

Then came a question that surprised me. It was about the pageant's previous owner, Donald Trump.

"Do you think you would have still competed if he [still owned] the pageant?"

The question was one I'd thought about before but had never been asked in an interview. My gut reaction was, *This is a gotcha moment.* This question was meant to create a salacious headline or a viral video clip at my expense. Even though other interviewers would occasionally allude to Trump's ownership of the pageant, they steered clear of any direct inquiry about him.

I assumed the avoidance of questions about him was because of the polarizing figure he was as sitting president of the United States. Perhaps he also wasn't asked about because of his controversial exit from pageantry four years earlier. Either way, there was little positive conversation to have about him as it related to the Miss Universe Organization. Injecting him into the dialogue was like asking someone about her divorce that happened five years ago. It was a touchy subject, and unless it produced a new and newsworthy revelation, there was no need to bring it up.

This interview was starkly different from any other because of its comprehensive nature. Its depth and breadth far outpaced almost every other one I'd done. Therefore, it made sense that at some point in time, a thorough production team—and interviewer like the one I sat in front of—would ask the unaskable question. I didn't consider that in the moment, though. I thought I was being ambushed. And while I had an answer, I didn't want to risk it being chopped and edited, taken out of context, or misunderstood. I decided to reply with a nonanswer.

"I'm not sure," I responded.

The interviewer quietly stared at me for a moment, both of us letting silence fill the room.

People don't like silence and will often try to fill it, whether in interviews or in depositions—formal interviews of witnesses under oath, typically in preparation for trial. Using silence is an effective strategy that interviewers, attorneys, therapists, and others sometimes use to glean additional information from people who don't want to divulge too much. When I was practicing law, if I asked a question and received a short answer or thought there was more to the response than the person was letting on, I would put my pen down and stare at the witness in silence. Sure, I could ask a follow-up question or ask the individual if they had anything else, but it would be too easy for them to say, "No, I have nothing else to say." Instead, I would opt to sit quietly and wait for them to fidget and squirm a little in the seat, then divulge more information just to fill the silence.

After using that strategy, I gained comfort with silence. I didn't know whether the interviewer was using the silent treatment on me, but whether she was or not, I wasn't going to give any more than I had.

Following a few moments of quiet, she ended our staring contest.

"Period," she said, chuckling a little.

"Yeah," I responded concisely, a weak smile on my face.

I wanted to say yes, pre-2015 and pre- his run for president, I would have competed in the Trump-owned pageant. In 2015, right before he made his reprehensible statements about Mexican immigrants, I'd competed in Miss North Carolina in the Miss America system and placed first runner-up in my last year of eligibility. I decided right away that the following year I'd compete in the Miss USA system. I wasn't paying much attention to politics, save for the big headlines and knowing who was running for president every four years. I was more focused on my excitement about an organization led by a female CEO, Paula Shugart, than I was on the callous owner of the organization.

The atmosphere then, before #MeToo forced accountability of sexual harassers, rapists, and the like, was intolerant of racism and xenophobia (to an extent) but would allow for a sprinkle of sexism, misogyny, and objectification if you were rich and well-liked, or if people agreed with you. This acquiescence to and acceptance of misogyny was something women understood we just had to deal with.

Before Trump ran for president, society generally viewed him as the kooky, brutish old white dude with no filter who was a real estate king in New York City. His famous catchphrase "You're fired!" from *The Apprentice* made him seem like a businessman who played it up for the cameras but knew his stuff. He made off-color comments about women and their looks and liked to wear beautiful women on his arm like props. But that was during a time when the general sentiment was that this was par for the course. Was his behavior really *that bad*? Yes. Was he going to be held accountable for it at the time? No.

In 2016, CNN published a 2005 interview Trump did with Howard Stern, in which he said he would walk into the dressing rooms of pageant contestants unannounced, so he could see them naked. Accounts from women who competed around that time confirm his admission. In 2016, this was a viral story. In 2005? There weren't any congressional hearings called. No big news of whistleblowers going public to report their boss's misdeeds. And even if there had been widespread outrage within his companies, would those feelings have been shared by the majority of the public? Sadly, awfully, likely no. And even if they had, would anything have changed?

Sitting in an interview in 2019, after Trump's rhetoric worsened and knowledge of it expanded, I decided that I wouldn't have competed if he'd still owned Miss USA.

While I wish each of us has the capacity to quit a job or refuse to apply when the employer is a rotten human being, I also try to understand the reality that exists when people have bills to pay, mouths to feed, and few alternate job prospects or time to search for other employment. It's easy for me to refuse to eat at a restaurant because of their position on social issues when I live in the heart of Manhattan with thousands of other restaurants to sweep by when I want a quick sandwich on the go. That decision may be much more difficult for someone who lives below the poverty line in a food desert with only one other restaurant and no grocery store for ten miles.

It's easy to tell women, if you don't want to be harassed, just don't compete. Let go of your dream to become Miss USA and the opportunities the title provides. Similarly, it's easy to tell us, if you don't want your husband to beat you, just leave. Or, if you don't want your boss to hit on you, just quit. The problem is that these responses accept the status quo and put the full responsibility of having a harassment-free life on the shoulders of victims, demanding that they make changes and adjustments to escape the consequences of harassment, domestic violence, and inequality. The better question is, Why did we allow a boss who harasses his employees to remain employed? Why did we look the other way when we saw evidence of domestic violence and justify our indifference with, "That's private family business"? And why did we as a society continue to enable and worship toxic masculinity incarnate? Why do we still?

Was our societal response pre-2015, or lack thereof, to men behaving badly a sign of the times? Perhaps. It's exactly why we need movements like #MeToo. So that even when the rich and famous and infamous think they aren't accountable to anyone because they don't have a boss, they become accountable to the public at large, who has refused—and will continue to refuse—to tolerate them.

I didn't want to answer for what Donald Trump had done. And I didn't want women who chose to compete in the pageant years ago—in spite of any fear or disgust or disagreement they had with the owner—feel like they needed to justify their choice. Too often, those who are most acutely harmed by bad behavior are asked to solve the problems themselves, when the demand should be of society as a whole to quit allowing bad behavior.

My reasoning, and my candid and complete answer to the question about Donald Trump, didn't fit in a tweet, a Facebook status, or a headline. So, when I was asked whether I would've competed with Donald Trump as the owner, I said, "I'm not sure."

Although I liked the final long-form video segment of the interview, I was frustrated and insulted after I saw the article headline about my answer: "Question about Trump stumps new Miss USA." A friend of mine texted me a link to the story and asked if I was okay. Okay? I was livid. I sent the information to Jackie immediately, who reached out to the outlet about the headline, which was soon changed to "Miss USA 'not sure' she would compete in Trump-owned pageant."

As angry as I was about feeling used for a clickbait headline, I was glad I'd trusted my instincts and remained tight-lipped with my response. If I'd said more, my guess is that my answer would have been mangled and twisted as much as my actual answer, just to give an outlet a few extra website hits. I'm also glad the experience gave me greater perspective as a journalist on the other side of the table.

Sometimes, even today, I get an unexpected response from a celebrity to a question I meant to be playful or innocuous. Once, at a movie premiere, I approached an actor who'd just had a viral fashion moment at a film festival because of an incredible and unique gown she wore. I asked her whether she looked forward to getting dressed up and walking the carpet for premieres as much as she looked forward to watching the movie. I was hoping she'd say she loves getting dressed up or enjoys the creative process with her team meticulously styling her, or maybe she'd talk about fashion as a form of self-expression.

Instead, she said something along the lines of, "I'm really looking forward to seeing this movie tonight," completely ignoring the crux of my question. I really wanted to know if she liked the fashion part of premieres as much as the film part, especially when she'd have to attend several premieres for the same movie. I didn't blame her, though. She didn't know me or my employer. Even though we don't deploy ambush questions or gotcha moments, she couldn't be expected to know which outlets she could trust and which outlets were going to twist an "I love fashion" answer into a headline like, "Movie star prefers fashion to film, can't stand annoying screenings." Even though I don't ever want or intend to be a part of twisting someone's words in that way, I get it. I've been there, and I get it.

Chapter 11

FACING THE UNIVERSE

With the addition of *Extra* interviews and red-carpet events to my calendar, I was busier than I'd ever been as Miss USA. It felt like I had three jobs: being Miss USA, doing correspondent work, and preparing for Miss Universe. If I wasn't sitting in movie screenings to prepare for a red carpet, writing a speech for an upcoming keynote, or hopping onto a plane during my nation-wide tour with Dress for Success, I was stressing about my Miss Universe preparation.

I visited a nutritionist the organization was connected to, secured a designer in South Carolina to design and construct my interview outfit, started working anew with Heather Sumlin on onstage question and interview prep, and returned to reading daily news briefings. I'd been reading *The Skimm* for years but figured adding the *New York Times* daily briefing email couldn't hurt either.

MUO also connected me with the organization's official gown sponsor. When I competed at Miss USA, every contestant was required to wear a gown from one dress designer, Sherri Hill. The gowns weren't free, and although we had some freedom when it came to the design of the dress, there were quite a few limitations—something I didn't fully grasp until after I'd won.

The person who won Miss USA was required to wear a dress from the same gown sponsor at the Miss Universe competition.

Five months before Miss USA, my state directors and I had flown to the gown sponsor's showroom to create a custom dress with the founder. I was ecstatic. I'd been competing in pageants for years by then, and every time I saw a local or state pageant, I could easily tell which gowns came from Sherri Hill. They were always among the most beautiful gowns, and many women who won state and local titles donned "a Sherri" on their crowning night.

When I arrived and had the opportunity to meet Sherri Hill herself, a legend in pageant land, I liked her. I appreciated that she was direct and candid during the design process. I told her I wanted a unique gown. Something with a cape. And probably an unexpected color. I vividly remember her looking at me and saying something to this effect: "You're North Carolina, right? Based on the dresses I've designed so far and where your state is in the alphabet, if you want a cape, you'll be about the seventh girl to wear one. Now, I hear you want something *unique . . .*" I appreciated the heads-up and immediately nixed the cape idea.

Sherri led me to her showroom and pointed out a gown that had a beautiful gold, silver, and diamante beaded detail around the shoulders. I told her I loved the beading, and she took to her sketch pad, drawing a one-shoulder gown with a high slit and a bead detail at the shoulder that wrapped from the front of my right shoulder, draped down my arm past my triceps, almost to my elbow, and connected to the fabric on the back of my right shoulder, with more beads dripping straight down from the back of my shoulder to my hip. I initially wanted the gown in a rich, deep-burgundy, velvet fabric that I thought would be unexpected, but was relieved that Sherri's team was happy to oblige a color change when I changed my mind shortly after leaving the showroom. After the dress arrived and went through some alterations and additions to the beaded shoulder detail, it was perfect.

Even though I enjoyed the simplicity of my Miss USA gown, it had been a strategic choice. I thought having a gown that wasn't decked out in crystals would help me to stand out because I expected that most women at the competition would opt for heavily beaded or fully beaded dresses. I also didn't want my dress to take the focus away from me—my big, bold hair or my face. Miss Universe was a whole different ball game. Sure, most of the women had tons of beads on their dresses, but these weren't just sparkly gowns. Every single year, women showed up in custom couture dresses worth tens of thousands of dollars.

Simplicity was my strategy for Miss USA, but I did an about-face for Miss Universe and wanted to be a walking disco ball. I wanted something over-the-top, bold, and unique. Unfortunately, executing that vision was much easier said than done. I'd begun my Miss Universe design meetings with Sherri and her team several weeks after I'd won Miss USA. We'd FaceTime and talk through some of my thoughts, I'd show her screenshots from Pinterest, and she'd walk through her showroom to show me elements from different gowns she had created. We both sketched dresses that we liked on me.

I don't remember when I became frustrated by the process, but I'm sure it was rather early on. Almost every time I pitched an idea or design element, or showed Sherri a sketch, she pointed out a problem with it.

I wanted a flesh-colored gown with a bustle piece that had blue or green crystals on part of it, and she pointed out that the crystal design would look strange on the bustle if the crystals were blue or green.

I wanted a fully beaded gown with a high slit that would narrow at my hip, cross my torso at the middle of my chest, then end at the shoulder opposite the slit. She informed me that there was no way to hold the dress together with the slit—flesh-colored mesh fabric wasn't strong enough. She didn't suggest alternatives to make the slit work and shot down the alternatives I inquired about.

I asked for a gown that would be a replica of my Miss USA gown, except it would be fully beaded instead of made of white velvet fabric, and the beads hanging from my shoulder would hit the ground rather than end at my hip. She told me the beads would tangle when I walked in the dress. A week after I suggested the design, my roommate wore a gown with the beaded detail I wanted. She walked onstage in the gown at a pageant she was appearing at overseas and did a full turn in the gown. The beads swung right into place when she finished.

I wasn't asking for impossible features, and I began to get the sense that I was asking for features that perhaps Sherri didn't want to do.

We continued our back-and-forth until New York Fashion Week in September. Sherri and many from her team were in town to show her collection, which would present me with the opportunity to see her in person and try on some of the dresses she had brought with her for that event. When what had become an almost routine exchange of me suggesting ideas and her shooting them down started up again, my patience finally broke.

I wanted to scream at her and ask why she couldn't just let someone else make my dress if she didn't want to do it. Sherri was providing the gowns for free in addition to her sponsorship of the organization, but at that point, I would've rather paid someone, anyone, to make me a custom dress than continue the process with her. I even asked my boss if I could find a different designer. My challenge was that I knew that Sherri Hill was a valuable sponsor for the organization, and I didn't want to be the person to destroy an important relationship. My frustration and anger brought tears to my eyes, and I asked Sherri, voice quivering, why she couldn't work with me to find a way to make a dress I wanted rather than giving me one hundred reasons why each of my suggestions wouldn't work.

After my feeble outburst, Sherri completely switched course during the session. Every time I asked about a gown feature or design element, she'd reply shortly, "Sure, we can do that," "Yes," or "Mhmm." I feared she was merely going along to get along and that she'd take my requests and deliver them the way she wanted on the back end.

As I started pulling dresses I thought were unique, I found one that was covered in jagged mirror pieces. It was a change of pace from the racks of fully beaded gowns in front of me that were beautiful but, in my opinion, fell short of some of the one-of-a-kind couture dresses I knew I'd see at Miss Universe. I saw potential in this dress, though, and hoped that picking something Sherri had already created and making a few changes to it would be a fair compromise—rather than continuing to push for an inventive dress that I felt she didn't want to invest time and resources into making.

● ● ●

Life has taught me that God has a plan for each of us, and his plan is perfect. His plan is unimpeachable. His timing is always right. And none of us are powerful enough to mess up the plan.

When I competed in 2015 at Miss North Carolina in the Miss America system, using my final year of eligibility, I held hands with a woman named Kate Peacock while we listened for the announcement of the winner. We were the final two, and while Kate had had a confident response to her onstage question minutes before, I didn't feel confident about how my own response had come across. As the host shouted Kate's name into the microphone, I walked forward to receive my first runner-up flowers, wishing I could have given my onstage question another shot and never wanting to be first runner-up ever again. I was angry at myself for getting so close and failing, devastated that I'd never get another chance at the crown.

That night, my mom helped me take my belongings back to my apartment, which wasn't far from the competition venue. She held my hand while I cried myself to sleep, still dressed in my evening gown from the pageant a few hours before.

The next year, I competed at Miss North Carolina USA. When I didn't capture the title in 2016 either, I threw myself into my studies and was scouted by the coach, who happened to be a lab professor for my trial advocacy class, for one of Wake Forest's trial teams. He convinced me to join his team, and we went on to win a national trial team tournament that year, the first time Wake Law had ever won.

The following year, in 2017, I competed at Miss North Carolina USA again. Failing to crack the top five this time, I considered forgoing my final year of eligibility. Instead of spending my time prepping for Miss USA, my loss cleared the way for me to devote myself to working for a pro bono client whose case my stepdad— also an attorney—and I had decided to take on. A few years later, in the summer of 2021, our client was freed after having spent over two decades of his life in prison for a low-level drug crime.

That same year, I started a blog for women's workwear fashions and began to volunteer for the Charlotte arm of a global organization called Dress for Success, which helps women achieve economic independence through a suiting program, financial literacy education, mock interview sessions, and other programs.

All of my losses taught me lessons and created opportunity for experiences that came together at just the right time.

My 2015 first runner-up loss motivated my onstage question preparation that propelled me into two answers on national television that were the best responses I'd ever given. Losing the first year I competed at NC USA opened the door for my participation on a history-making trial team that I wouldn't have joined had I captured the crown. My loss the second time around came right before I dove into pro bono work, a fashion blog, and volunteerism for Dress for Success, each of which became defining parts of my "brand" that I pitched to the judges at state the following year at Miss USA, and that I talked about throughout my reign. My choice to compete a third time was motivated by the fear of once again feeling the regret I couldn't shake at not having given my full self to track and field, failing to advance to nationals, and the what-ifs that crowded my mind for years after that. If I was going to lose, I needed to know I had done my very best, rather than spend the rest of my life wondering if I could've finally made it happen.

After I won Miss USA, I became a Global Impact Ambassador for Dress for Success and received countless interview requests and features based on my pro bono work, criminal justice reform advocacy, and fashion advice for the workplace—all skills, knowledge, and experience I'd gained following my losses.

Most importantly, my win at Miss USA in May 2019 placed me squarely within a group that received global attention, since it was the first time Black women could see themselves holding some of the most prestigious and well-known pageant titles simultaneously. If I'd won years earlier, I wouldn't have been as strong a competitor, and I would have missed out on becoming a part of history.

When my mascara was streaking down my face, tears loosening the glue on my fake eyelashes while I sobbed after losing Miss North Carolina on my final try in 2015, I had no idea what was waiting for me four years in the future. But God did. He had a plan that defied the bounds of my own imagination. And as I continued my preparation for the biggest pageant I would ever compete in, I gripped tightly to my trust in his plan. I couldn't ruin it. I also knew that if winning Miss Universe wasn't a part of that plan, it was because he was preparing me for something even more earth-shattering.

• • •

I landed in Atlanta, Georgia, seven pieces of matching luggage in tow, for the Miss Universe Competition. I arranged my baggage and asked one of the staff members who was picking me up to take a photo of me with my suitcases. The iconic I-just-arrived-at-Miss-Universe photos were something I'd been looking forward to taking since I'd won Miss USA. I stood in my pink, pointed-toe boots, pink suit, and giant faux fur coat next to my luggage and smiled for a photo I later captioned, "Just touched down in the A for a work trip. Trying to get a promotion."

If the Miss USA Competition was a carnival, Miss Universe was Cirque du Soleil. The number of contestants almost doubled, fans were gathered around the hotel waiting to glimpse the representative from their favorite country, and countless staff were available to capture content, direct contestants on where to go, approve our competition wardrobes, and shuffle us from venue to venue for various events.

By Miss Universe standards, this was a brief competition— only ten days from registration day to finals night. Ten days to do fittings, photoshoots, sponsor meetings, and interviews. Ten days to learn walking patterns, practice dance routines for the live television show, and participate in the preliminary competition. Somehow, the organizers also planned to give women flying in from all over the world a glimpse of Atlanta via tours and activities squeezed in between meals. The competition was a blur.

I enjoyed meeting the women representing the other eighty-nine countries competing for the title, but I was also "hangry" a lot of the time. Miss Universe was my version of the Olympics, and I wanted my body to be in the best shape it had ever been in, which meant I'd put myself on an extremely restrictive diet, save for an occasional bite-size serving of a dessert on my Saturday cheat day. This control was a big challenge for a girl who could eat dessert with every meal and some more in between.

My favorite part of the competition was our gift exchange, when most of the competitors would give gifts from their countries to the other contestants. It was a way for us to meet each other and get a small taste of one another's cultures. I gave my fellow contestants an American flag pin, a small token representing an iconic global symbol. Miss Brazil gifted everyone a silver necklace with a pendant that said *Sorte*, which means "luck" in Portuguese. Miss Croatia gave us palm-size heart ornaments that said *Zagreb* on them, which is the capital of Croatia. The hearts were similar to Licitar cookies, a popular cake treat in Croatia historically exchanged as an expression of love. Miss China handed out tiny panda dolls and magic Chinese paper art tumbling flowers, both of which I keep in my desk to this day and play with occasionally.

Before I knew it, interview day had arrived. I felt more prepared than I'd ever been in my life. I'd researched each of the judges and practiced interview and onstage questions nearly every day as I approached the competition. I wore an all-white custom suit that made me feel like a goddess. I walked in with a plan. I wanted the judges to know three things about me: I'm an attorney, I have a fashion blog, and I volunteer for Dress for Success.

I walked out knowing I'd executed the plan but wondered if adhering so closely to it was a mistake. Did my preparedness read as contrived? Did my confidence in my hard work read as arrogance and expectation that I'd make the finals, since the competition was being held in my own country? Almost every single question I heard from the judges was one I'd thought about, answered in practice rounds, or answered in a competition before. I left the interview room and told my coach it was either the best interview I'd ever done in my life or it was an interview the judges would read as manufactured, forced, or inauthentic. I wondered, *Maybe I prepared too much?*

Once that interview was over, though, I had to put the day behind me, focus on the preliminary competition ahead of me, and look toward finals shortly after, all of which came in a flash. We started finals day with a dress rehearsal, which would be the first time each of us would get to see each other's finals night outfits. I'd met Miss South Africa, Zozi Tunzi, months before the competition and really liked her. Throughout the competition itself, we were frequently put in groups together, and she always made me laugh. In the evening gown formation in our dress rehearsal, she was standing directly to the left of me, and when I saw her dress, I thought it was one of the most unique, creative, and beautiful garments I'd seen in a long time.

Silver liquid beading draped around her shoulders, starting at an embellished neckpiece and blending down into gold and then rich, deep-blue liquid beads. The same colors repeated in beading attached to her dress, starting around her waist and flowing down to the floor. It was a stunning dress—my favorite in the competition—and I told her as much.

Her dress was everything I had wanted my dress to be—inventive, stunning, luxe. But as I looked into the oversized mirrors positioned on the sides of the stage, I realized that the dress I wore wasn't the same one I'd seen in the mirror at the Miss Universe office. I'd loved the dress I'd tried on a couple of weeks before. It was initially supposed to be my gown for the preliminary competition, but I thought it was edgy and would stand out during finals, so I switched the two. I wanted a nude-illusion dress, so it would look like the jagged, gold-mirrored pieces were the only items on my body. I therefore asked Sherri and her team to use a fabric color that would match my skin tone.

When the dress arrived, it was about three shades too light, which wasn't a complete surprise because Sherri had once compared my skin tone to someone on her staff who appeared to be a blonde-haired white woman. I'd asked her team if they could dye the fabric to match my skin tone. They told me it wasn't possible, which wasn't a big issue when I saw the dress during my fitting in the overhead office lighting at the Miss Universe styling room where I tried it on. Unfortunately, under stage lights, the fabric that didn't match my skin color was highlighted by the dark ceiling and seating area reflecting into the mirrored parts of my dress, so the mirrored parts alternated between looking dark and metallic like the floor, and bright and metallic like the white stage lights (a potential issue I vaguely remembered Sherri telling me about). The fabric made it look like dress lining was poking through—lining that you weren't supposed to see.

Worse still, Miss Puerto Rico had worn a gold metallic dress covered with similar metallic shards during the preliminary competition days before, and as I looked over to find her during dress rehearsal, I saw that she was wearing it again. Many women end up wearing different dresses for prelims and finals, so I was surprised to see her in the same gown. I was particularly uneasy to see it since the voiceover track that would play while I walked in evening gown, if I advanced that far in the competition, was supposed to be me talking about how unique my dress was. Now I'd be in the competition with someone who was wearing my gown's cousin.

My reaction as I looked at my dress in the stage mirrors was, *This isn't it.* As I walked off the stage at the end of dress rehearsal, I had a decision to make: wear the gown I had on, or wear something else. I'd left my preliminary dress option at the hotel instead of bringing it to the auditorium, because I knew the mirror dress would be a risk and I'd want the option of backing out at the last minute. But I wanted to believe I could beg and convince someone to bring my other dress to the auditorium if I really needed it. *Would it be worth it?*

I decided I needed to be in a positive headspace and not worry or wonder about a plan God had already worked out. If I was supposed to win, nothing was going to stop me, especially not a dress. I could not allow myself to be distracted by another woman wearing a similar dress, nor by a daring hairstyle I tried for the first time in competition. (My hair wasn't good, and it wasn't the fault of the stylist either. She had done exactly what I'd asked her to do.)

If I wasn't supposed to win, if it wasn't God's plan for me, the most beautiful, most expensive, out-of-this-world dress wasn't going to help. Neither would the preliminary competition dress sitting in my hotel room.

I walked back to the dressing room after our rehearsal and started getting ready for the competition that would take place later that night.

• • •

My hands gripped the handle of my carry-on luggage as I somberly dragged it to an airport lounge. I was exhausted, having stayed up most of the night with my family at a local diner after the pageant. The highlight of the final Miss Universe competition was looking into the audience and seeing my mom, dad, stepdad, siblings, grandparents, and closest friends cheering for me while I advanced all the way to the top ten out of ninety countries. I was disappointed to stand onstage in the evening gown I'd taken a risk on and watch the fifth woman hear the name of her country called. I was cut right after the evening gown competition.

I wondered, but I never reached out to the judges to ask, what had kept me from advancing. Getting an answer to my question wasn't going to change anything. You only get one shot at Miss Universe, and I'd blown mine. I didn't know if it was something I said or didn't say in the interview. I didn't know if it was my stage performance or my wardrobe. I just knew I wasn't selected.

Three things gave me peace.

First, I really liked Zozi. She was her authentic self throughout the competition. She didn't behave differently in front of pageant officials versus behind the scenes when it was just us contestants. She was laid-back and wasn't constantly fronting for social media or fans. During the competition, she spoke profound and insightful truths about the importance of representation. We needed a dark-skinned, bold queen with short, coarse hair to be the face and voice for Black women at Miss Universe. She was all that and more, and I was genuinely happy for her when she won.

Second, I had given my all to prepare for the competition. Even though I hadn't grown up wanting to be Miss Universe the same way I ached to be Miss USA, the fierce competitor in me wanted to win it because it's the most prominent, widely known, televised international pageant. I knew the broader reach and audience for Miss Universe, compared to Miss USA, was an undeniable benefit of winning.

Third, although it hurt to lose, I knew God had something else in store for me. I had wanted winning Miss Universe to be part of the plan, but since it wasn't, I was ready to find out what was.

Chapter 12

SISTERHOOD

When I was an undergraduate, I'd wanted to pledge a sorority. I saw the togetherness and immediate bond sorority sisters enjoyed. I wanted that—I wanted to belong.

I'd set my sights on one of the five in the Divine Nine, the historically Black sororities and fraternities that made up the National Pan-Hellenic Council. Part of my desire came from wanting to wear the swaggy clothes with iconic colors and letters. *Paraphernalia.* The meaning and history behind the letters intrigued me as well.

By the time I was ready and had saved up enough money to afford it, the sorority I'd selected had a mandatory initial meeting, scheduled the same day as an out-of-town track meet. As a scholarship athlete, I wasn't about to miss a travel trip. I missed out on joining the sorority and never revisited the topic.

Lucky for me, the Miss USA sisterhood brought some of the togetherness and belonging I craved. Around the other women, I felt the same warmth as I did when I was home with my parents and my five siblings. Susie Castillo, Miss USA 2003, talked to me about her days as an actor and MTV host. Nia Sanchez, Miss USA 2014, reached out to me every time she was in New York, bubbling with positivity and gentle guidance. Deshauna Barber,

Miss USA 2016, gave me an inside look at her career as a public speaker and told me how she'd signed with her speakers' bureau and manager. Olivia Jordan, Miss USA 2015, seemed to have a sixth sense for when I needed a bit of encouragement and was one of my biggest cheerleaders throughout my reign.

Sarah Rose Summers, Kara McCollough, Erin Brady, Rima Fakih, Tara Conner, Shanna Moakler, Kenya Moore, Nana Meriwether, Alyssa Campanella, Chelsea Cooley, Kandace Kreuger, and countless others gave me advice, a kind word, and some of their time during my reign. It felt like a sorority, a sisterhood of women I'd looked up to and idolized for years who became my allies and friends because of our shared experience of being Miss USA.

Thankfully, the sisterhood extended even beyond Miss USA titleholders. The Miss Universe Organization ran Miss Universe, Miss Teen USA, and Miss USA when I won, so I joined a trio of MUO titleholders. Miss Teen USA, Kaliegh, didn't live in the titleholder apartment with Cat and me, but we stayed in touch between joint appearances. Even though Cat was constantly flying all over the world, when she and I were in NYC at the same time, she'd invite me out to dinner so we could catch up. She'd show me new places in the city and answer all the questions I was afraid to ask people in the organization. She made me feel welcome. And I wanted to pass that welcome feeling along to Zozi.

Things started off quickly when Zozi's flight arrived in New York. Esther brought her into the apartment, and we showed her around before giving her some time to unpack and relax in her room before the circus started up again. Zozi did plenty of press, but barely a week after her win, Toni-Ann Singh of Jamaica won the Miss World title, expanding the trio of titleholders of color—Kaliegh, Nia, and me—to a quartet with Zozi, and then to a quintet with Toni-Ann. CNN, *E! News Daily Pop*, *Good Morning America*, and plenty of other media outlets started up the rounds of interviews again, which turned Zozi's solo celebration into a win for us all. I invited Nia over to the apartment one night to hang out with Zozi and me, since we were doing so many interviews together. A selfie the three of us took together and posted on our Instagram stories made its way to TMZ and other outlets. "Miss USA & Miss America Welcome Miss Universe in NYC for Historic Girls' Night!!!" the headline screamed.

I wanted to make sure Zozi felt comfortable living in a new country she'd only visited twice before, one of those times which had been for the competition that made her Miss Universe. She didn't have a proper coat that would help her survive a New York winter, so I took her to a local department store to make sure she had one that was warm enough. We made the rounds at a few of my favorite restaurants, and I helped her figure out how to unlock our tricky front door.

Beyond celebrating with my fellow queens, I was also celebrating being done with my ridiculous diet. My sweet tooth had been begging to be fed for a while, and I took full advantage of not having to worry about a swimsuit competition again. At the time, the Miss Universe Organization would purchase groceries for us each week, and I'd created a grocery list in the notes app on my phone weeks before the Miss Universe Competition.

Nutella, whipped cream, cookie dough ice cream, cookie dough, chocolate chips, mango ice cream, chips and salsa, bagels, Oreos, and tons of other foods I'd been avoiding altogether or eating only on my cheat day filled my grocery order after the competition. My colleagues who weren't on the food order group chat noticed that I was off my diet when they asked for a Starbucks order before a group interview. My "short" (a size smaller than the "tall") vanilla chai tea latte had turned into a tall white hot chocolate with a warmed-up brownie on the side.

I binged so much that I gained a solid thirteen pounds in two weeks between the end of the Miss Universe competition and the beginning of winter vacation with my family. I didn't own a scale at the time, but I'd weighed myself in the gym at the competition hotel when I was at 127 pounds. (Pretty tiny for me, considering that I'm five foot six and have a naturally muscular build. I was a size zero/two.) Then I weighed myself again, at the gym in the hotel where my family was staying in Orlando for our biannual Christmas trip to Universal Studios. I saw the scale hit 140 and cackled. During the vacation, I posed for a photo in my swimsuit by the pool and was convinced I looked the same as I did during the competition. That's when I stopped trusting scales.

My sugar intake increased dramatically, and so did my bookings for work with *Extra*. Upon returning to NYC on December 9 after the competition, I unpacked my nearly three hundred pounds of luggage, did some interviews with Zozi and Kaliegh, and got right back into the swing of things.

- December 14: I interviewed Salma Hayek, Tiffany Haddish, Rose Byrne, Billy Porter, and Jennifer Coolidge about their new movie, *Like a Boss*.
- December 15: I talked to Jamie Foxx, Michael B. Jordan, and Bryan Stevenson about their movie *Just Mercy*.
- December 16: I was on a red carpet for the movie *Bombshell*, talking to Charlize Theron and Kate McKinnon.
- December 18: I sat down with Helen Hunt and Paul Reiser to discuss a *Mad About You* reboot.

Of course, I still had appearances and interviews of my own to do while all of this played out. So, after heading to Connecticut on December 19 to watch Nia crown the new Miss America, I was grateful to have a couple of weeks off to go home and visit my family.

Holidays are important for my tight-knit family. I'd skipped celebrating Thanksgiving with them since it was the day I flew to Atlanta for the Miss Universe competition, so I was looking forward to some uninterrupted time at home over Christmas. I loved doing interviews with *Extra*, but I love my family more, so I asked Esther to block off my schedule the entire time I was home. I didn't want to return to New York early or travel anywhere for an interview. I just wanted to hang out with my family. I was surprised, therefore, to hear from Esther about potentially doing an interview during those two weeks.

"Hey, *Extra* called. They want to know if you can do an interview on January 3," she said.

"Mmmm," I mused. "I wish I could, but I'll actually be down in Florida then with my family."

"Well, funny that you say that, because the interview is scheduled to happen in Florida," she responded. I knew Esther took free time and family vacations seriously, so I was surprised she'd called and was a little taken aback that she was gently pushing the interview. *Hmm, must be important*, I thought.

Wanting to be helpful, I told her, "Well, maybe if the interview is close by, I could sneak away for a few hours, but I really don't want to spend the whole day on it."

I hadn't been able to spend time with my family in months, and I didn't know when the next time was that I'd have this long to hang out with everyone. With my five siblings, niece, stepdad, and mom on the trip, you can imagine how hard it had been to sync everyone's schedules.

"Okay, that's fair," Esther said. "I'll find out how far it is from where you'll be and call you right back."

"Thanks, E. By the way, do you know who the interview is for?" I asked.

"No, but it sounded pretty important when they asked me about it. I'll find out."

I was secretly hoping the interview would be in Miami or some other place that was far enough from Orlando for me to justify turning it down. I generally make work a high priority, but after missing Thanksgiving and having such a hectic schedule before and after Miss Universe, I was ready for some uninterrupted time with the fam.

I held my breath after answering Esther's phone call, listening to what she'd found out.

"It looks like the venue would be a quick plane ride or a few hours' drive from Orlando," she told me.

Dammit.

"Okay," I paused, wondering if I could still reasonably turn it down. "Who is it? The interview—who is it with?"

"Oprah."

I blinked a couple of times, pressing the phone a bit harder against my ear.

"As in . . . Winfrey?"

"That's the one!" Esther laughed.

"Well then, uh, wow, um," I stuttered, laughing in disbelief. "I guess I could make that work!"

• • •

After the Oprah interview, which turned out to be for her 2020 Vision tour for WW (formerly Weight Watchers) and the end of winter vacation for my family, life shifted into high gear once again. My red carpets and interviews for *Extra* continued, appearances and media for Miss USA ramped back up, and I honed my plans for what I'd do after my reign ended.

The typical length for a titleholder's reign is one year. Since I'd won on May 2, 2019, I guessed that Miss USA 2020 would be held sometime in May 2020. MUO helped me to set up meetings with agencies during a trip to LA, when I was helping cover the Oscars for *Extra*, and I found an agent I liked at WME. By then, we'd begun hearing reports about a contagious virus that was ravaging China. They were calling it the "coronavirus." I didn't have any plans to visit Asia, so while I cautiously followed the story, I didn't feel like I was in serious or imminent danger.

Shortly after I returned to NYC, I was readying for another round of travel and appearances. It was March 12, and the number of coronavirus cases in the state was on a dangerous upward trend. The first case was reported on March 1, and by the twelfth, there were well over two hundred cases. The governor of New York declared a state of emergency, and the caution I'd felt earlier in the year began to turn to dread.

At 9:00 a.m. I checked my phone to see a text from Esther, who told me that a Dress for Success event in Ohio I was due to attend the following week had been cancelled. I loved volunteering for DFS and was disappointed that I was going to miss out, but it was only the first in a string of events to unfold that day. Soon afterward, a fashion show fundraiser in North Carolina I was supposed to walk in was delayed. A South Carolina school visit was cancelled. I was due to appear at a benefit concert that night in New York City and was looking forward to wearing a new outfit Emma had found for me, but the prospect of me getting dressed up in it was beginning to look unlikely. After not hearing from Esther following the latest cancellation, I shot her a text.

Hey! Concert still on for tonight?

Hold pls.

Esther was juggling appearances and events for Zozi, Kaliegh, and me, and plans were constantly changing as the virus continued to spread. She was also helping me coordinate acting lessons with a local school, the American Musical and Dramatic Academy.

Kk. Also, session today with acting teacher went well. AMDA is closed starting next week though and will be doing virtual classes after that. I told her I'd talk to you about scheduling our next meeting, I responded.

Barely an hour later, I received an update on my phone from the *New York Times* app: "New York State is banning most gatherings of more than 500 people, including Broadway shows, to curb the spread of the coronavirus."

It was the first time I felt like the world was closing in on me. Sure enough, when Esther called the concert venue after the news update, the status of the event had changed.

Cancelled.

Over the next few days, the situation became more and more dire. There was a run on grocery stores. Toilet paper was sold out everywhere, which was particularly inconvenient because Zozi and I happened to be down to our last roll. My mom mailed us some, and our boss, Paula Shugart, brought us some from her apartment. Hygienic, surgical-type gloves and most cleaning supplies were out of stock at stores. We didn't know how the virus was transmitted, so when Zozi and I went shopping for groceries (there were no delivery slots available), we were told to wipe all of them down before putting them away in the refrigerator or the cupboard.

By March 21, the number of coronavirus cases in New York had increased from two hundred to over ten thousand, and the state accounted for one third of all coronavirus infections in the country. On the night of the twenty-second, a stay-at-home order was enacted by New York's governor, closing all nonessential businesses in the state.

The world outside my apartment had been incrementally slowing down over the previous week, but after the stay-at-home order, the streets resembled a ghost town. My bedroom window overlooked bustling Sixth Avenue, and I would usually wake up early each morning to the beeping of car horns, the growl of delivery trucks, and other loud but comforting sounds of the city. On the morning of the twenty-third, the street was unrecognizably quiet. I had never experienced the Manhattan I was now seeing, and I didn't like it.

The governor announced that all schools in the state would remain closed for two weeks, so we assumed the stay-at-home order would be in place for about the same length of time. As unfathomable as the halting of one of the fastest-moving cities in the world was, it was more tangible to imagine it when we knew it would only last for two weeks—like a two-week vacation none of us expected. Two weeks. That was doable.

Of course, the stay-at-home order lasted longer than two weeks.

Now, years after the pandemic started, it seems naïve to have believed the stay-at-home order and chaos would only last two weeks. But I've never in my lifetime known a comparable event that shut down the entire world so completely. After the first order was extended through mid-April, we understood. COVID-19, which we were still calling the "coronavirus," was spiraling out of control, and New York seemed to be bearing the brunt of it. My family, home in the Carolinas, routinely checked in on me, their worry palpable through text messages and phone calls asking for details about how I was holding up. We all assumed things would calm down soon, since people largely weren't leaving their homes.

But the infections kept multiplying. And the deaths kept increasing. A hospital was set up in Central Park, and the stay-at-home order was extended for an additional two weeks, until the end of April. Then another two weeks was added. Then three weeks. Somehow, what I genuinely believed was two weeks away from life as I knew it had turned into spending my reign sequestered in an apartment through June. However, my having to stay at home seemed trivial in the face of tens of thousands of deaths of people around the world from a virus we still didn't understand.

In-person appearances and events turned into a constant churn of social media content and Instagram or Facebook Live sessions on the official titleholder accounts. It wasn't easy remaining positive and sharing uplifting messages to viewers when the world around Zozi and me felt like it was melting. Keeping our eyes focused on gratitude made it a little easier. Neither of us contracted COVID, despite venturing maskless into Manhattan early in the pandemic for groceries before we knew the virus was airborne. We were stuck indoors, sure, but we lived in an enormous three-bedroom, three-bathroom apartment with an office, sizeable foyer, living room, small sitting room area, dining room, and full kitchen. We didn't have to pay for rent, and Miss Universe continued paying our salaries throughout our respective reigns.

Not everything was going well, though. A combination of being stuck indoors, not drinking enough water, not removing my makeup effectively enough each day, and eating more processed foods than ever wreaked havoc on my skin. I was thankful not to have any in-person events, since my forehead, cheeks, and chin were breaking out like I'd never seen before.

Worse yet, despite the stay-at-home orders, the world hadn't completely stopped, and news of the murders of Ahmaud Arbery, Breonna Taylor, and George Floyd sparked the largest, most comprehensive protest movements of my lifetime. The resurgence of the Black Lives Matter movement assimilated people across the country in a way that was encouraging to see. Zozi and I knew we needed to add our voices to the rally cries. I went to a protest with a friend of mine and documented the process for *Extra* to air. Initially, I wasn't sure what the reaction of the Miss Universe Organization would be. The protest I went to happened just before a conference call I had with Paula, Esther, and Zozi. I hadn't made it back to the apartment before the call began, and when Paula and Esther asked where I had been, I told them.

"I just went to a Black Lives Matter protest."

Paula paused. "How was it?" she asked.

"Incredible! I feel so motivated and alive. It felt amazing to chant and shout. We were walking through the streets, from Times Square past Grand Central Station, headed toward the East River, stopping traffic. 'Whose streets? *Our streets!*' It was mind-blowing!" I realized I was rambling.

"Wow," Paula responded. "If I was still in New York, I would've gone with you."

Paula didn't know that four years earlier, I'd bought a sweatshirt that had "Black Lawyers Matter" printed across the front. I loved that sweatshirt but seldom wore it. I remember removing a social media post from 2013, when I'd worn my "Black Lawyers Matter" sweatshirt. I was aware that far too many people thought BLM was a violent, radical group and often didn't agree with its ideas. I was still competing in pageants, and I worried about the possibility that pageant judges would look at my Instagram, see photos of me wearing the sweatshirt, and think twice about crowning me. Years later, having this kind of support from MUO, an organization I'd worked for years to have the chance to represent, was a heavenly feeling.

Zozi and I posted on our personal social media accounts in support of Black Lives Matter and the movement that was happening. Soon after, the official Miss Universe, Miss USA, and Miss Teen USA accounts were posting the same. I never would have imagined I'd see a pageant posting in support of Black Lives Matter, but now Miss USA's official account was posting it. Progress is possible.

The year 2020 was a whirlwind, and the pandemic was a difficult part of it, but one silver lining in the experience was the sisterhood that helped me through it. From mid-March to the end of the year, Zozi and I saw each other every day. We checked on each other, carried each other through that uncertain time, and shared a closeness we didn't have with other titleholders. We protested together, did interviews together, had movie nights together, and often ordered food or dessert together. We had a sisterhood in a time of great need. Even though my introverted nature prefers living alone, having a roommate through the beginning of the pandemic was a need God fulfilled before I knew of the need myself.

The sisterhood that held me together didn't end with Zozi. The twice-weekly Instagram Live sessions that began with Zozi and me together soon extended into hosting various guests, most of whom were current or former state and national (and international for Zozi) titleholders. When we needed to connect with the Miss USA fan base, in a time when people wanted human connection and a break from loneliness, countless Miss USAs were willing to hop online for fifteen minutes to two hours to talk about the pandemic and their reigns, and share some inspiration to get all of us through. I had the opportunity to talk to the first Miss USA who was Black, Carole Gist, about her reign and its importance. Nurse Kelley Johnson gave us advice and insight into what she was going through as a medical worker and how we could keep ourselves and our loved ones safe. Tara Connor, "Mess USA," as she calls herself, got candid about some of the missteps in her reign, explaining how she learned from them and how that helped her achieve the life she enjoys today.

My pageant sisters were part of what kept me going in a time when I struggled to maintain my own positivity and sanity. It was the sorority I'd always wanted. One that tightened around me during an otherwise awful time.

Chapter 13

DETERMINING MY OWN DESTINY

Without any jet-setting, dinners, fundraisers, and media choking my schedule, the remainder of my reign crept by. The hours in each day seemed to expand. In some ways, the extra free time I had each day was driving me crazy, especially as a person who always had fire under her feet, happy to fill her days with commitments. Yet the extra time also forced me to make time for joy. Or to discover what joy actually was for me. I began constantly asking myself, *What makes you happy?*

I had spent much of my life focused on excelling and taking the next logical step in my life, whatever that step was, without much thought about whether that step was the one I would enjoy or look forward to. I was in high school when I decided to become an attorney. At seventeen years old, I was applying for colleges in-state, so I could afford law school after earning my undergraduate degree. After undergrad came law school and graduate business school, then passing the bar, then another bar, then life as an attorney. On May 1, 2019, I was a practicing attorney, living a life I'd laid out for myself as a kid more than a decade earlier. Suddenly, on May 2, I was thrust into a dream job, being Miss USA, a title fewer than seventy women *in history* at the time had won.

I felt I was facing an infinite span of opportunity, free to choose what my next step would be. As my reign came to a close, and I again faced the decision I'd made when I was a high schooler, it was with more possibility within reach than I'd ever envisioned. In deciding my next steps, I had a new dedication to dreaming big rather than thinking logically. Instead of asking myself what made sense, I asked myself what would make me happy. Not only as a career, but what could I do every single day to be happy? Work would be a part of that, but only a part, not the focus.

As I questioned myself, I found it wasn't always one big thing for me that filled my cup. It was a platter of little things. I used to find joy in accomplishment, in busyness. Now, I learned to find it in picking up a bouquet of flowers on my way back from a run to my favorite bakery, something trivial I wouldn't have previously made time for. I actually felt fulfillment when hopping down a Wikipedia- or TikTok-fueled rabbit hole about high diving or a true-crime story, or buying decor for my new, very expensive apartment.

A month and a half before the Miss USA 2020 Competition, at which I would crown the next titleholder, I moved out of the Miss Universe titleholder apartment and into my own place— one step toward life outside of the organization. MUO funded the move for each titleholder, ordering boxes, waiting for the title-holder to fill them, and then shipping them to all corners of the earth, depending on the destination. This was helpful, considering that between fees, deposits, and first month's rent for my midtown spot, I paid over $10,000 for my new apartment.

The cost didn't matter to me, though. While I was grateful for over a year of being Miss USA, I was also ready to move on. That fire under my feet was burning hotter by the minute. There were things I loved about being Miss USA and would miss. The people I worked with in the organization, like Esther and Paula. The digital and content team that was always chasing after me for past-due social media content. Waking up each morning and looking at the Mikimoto crown that sat on my nightstand.

There were also parts of being Miss USA that I was ready to put behind me. Feeling like I had no control over my schedule or final say in the events I did was one of them. Feeling stagnant was another. After not winning Miss Universe, I was eager to hop full throttle into my new career as a TV correspondent and host, but that was difficult to do when events conflicted with responsibilities I still held with the organization. However, one opportunity I wanted fit squarely within both desires: hosting Miss USA 2020.

I might have just begun my TV career, yet I'd done plenty of work hosting awards dinners and fundraisers, moderating panels, and doing live TV interviews. I wanted the chance to host on a larger scale and was confident I'd do well on the Miss USA telecast. I began by dropping hints. Then, in the months leading up to the date, I outright repeatedly asked to host the competition. Weeks before the competition, I was over the moon to find out I'd cohost finals night for Miss Teen USA, cohost the preliminary competitions for Miss USA and Miss Teen USA, and serve as a correspondent for the Miss USA final telecast. Sure, I felt some nerves, but I was operating in a space I'd lived in for years—pageantry. I'd get most of my nerves ironed out during dress rehearsals and the preliminary competitions. More importantly, the hosting I'd do at the competition felt like an appropriate transition, from the end of a reign I loved into the start of a career that felt right for me. And that, without question, made me happy.

• • •

The challenge in pageants is that oftentimes, more than one competitor is deserving of the title, but when the night is over, only one person can win. At the end of most state pageants I've attended, there's a top-five photo taken featuring the night's winner and her four runners-up. I've seen old photos that have five state titleholders in one picture: there's the winner that year with a crown on her head, and, depending on how old the photo is, the runners-up are women who win the following year and the year after and the year after, in that same state or in other states. Sometimes, the women who win later end up performing better at the Miss USA competition than the women who'd bested them years before.

The challenges occur in other settings too. Maybe you were passed up for a promotion this year, but that doesn't mean you weren't worthy. Sometimes it's just the wrong time. Sometimes growing and learning for another year or more gives you the time you need to prepare for difficulties you don't know about yet. Life will be okay without that promotion at this time. Believing that, living that, and continuing on the journey of achieving the thing meant for you takes nerve.

At the end of the 2020 Miss USA Competition, on my 557th day as Miss USA 2019, I stood onstage in Memphis, Tennessee, with fifty-one worthy women and crowned one of them. When I returned to my hotel suite, I was surrounded by family and friends who'd flown in to support me and celebrate with me. And sweat with me. I prefer to keep my hotel rooms (and my apartment) around seventy-three degrees and didn't think to turn down the thermostat to accommodate all the people who would be in my room until it was too late. We ended up having to leave the door open all night.

The following morning, I met Esther to return my Miss Universe cell phone, wiped clean and ready for the next user. Then I lugged my suitcases down the elevator and loaded myself into a car bound for the airport. My solo departure was a stark difference from the escort I'd had when I'd won, but it was a difference I appreciated. Then, I had been chaperoned into a new life, but now I was sauntering out of it under my own power, able to determine my own destiny day-to-day.

When I made it back to New York, I strode into my apartment building and picked up a large package from the doorman on my way in. I couldn't remember ordering anything on Amazon or placing an order for any boots, which would've explained the size and shape of the box. My suitcases were cluttering my kitchen, still bulging with clothes from the past week, when I opened the package and found a plaque. I'd ordered one weeks before but had forgotten about it. *Extra* had been nominated for an Emmy award, and even though we didn't win, nominees could order a plaque commemorating the nomination. Since I was one of the show's correspondents, I was eligible to order a plaque. It felt like a welcome gift to my new life. It was no Mikimoto crown, nor was it an Emmy award, but it was a wink to new possibilities, a reminder that I'd done a great deal but hadn't yet reached my ceiling.

The truth is, even as a *former* Miss USA, the pageantry never ends. My crown replicas sit on a shelf where my business and legal awards would have sat, had I remained in the legal profession or transitioned into a business role. I still select gowns to wear, but now they're for red carpets, awards ceremonies, and lavish fundraising dinners instead of pageant stages and appearances. Onstage questions have morphed into the average watercooler banter with colleagues about current events and the latest political race.

People call us pageant girls fake—our blinding white smiles, big hair, and ever-present positivity an act assembled to earn shallow and meaningless recognition. People also assume that their work distinguishes them from the parade of tall, slender, crown-donning women they envision when they think about pageants. None of that is true. Every one of us has practiced a little pageantry in our lives. We call it "sportsmanship" when we shake hands with the team that defeated us in a basketball tournament. It's labeled "professionalism" when we relegate outright anger at coworkers to passive-aggressive emails with the boss copied on the chain. The pageant wave after a win is the same one I've seen politicians use after a victory speech in front of a crowd, hand to the sky, waving at everyone and no one, sometimes holding their suit jacket closed with the opposite hand, the same way I gripped my bouquet of flowers in front of me when I won Miss USA.

Each of us is finding happiness, gaining life experience, and making a little space for ourselves in a crowded world. We just do it in separate arenas—and the pageant world happens to be more sparkly than most.

Cheslie and Kenya
Moore backstage
at a game show

Family trip to Orlando, FL, 2018 (Back row: Page, David, April, Asa, Cheslie, Chandler; Front row: Brooklyn, Raegan, Jet)

Cheslie and niece Raegan Kryst

LEFT: Raegan watching her Aunt Cheslie as she prepares to do the Oprah interview, Orlando, FL

BOTTOM: Cheslie interviewing Oprah Winfrey in January 2020

Photo courtesy of Extra

TOP: Different views of Cheslie's stunning Miss Universe pageant dress

BOTTOM: Cheslie and Zozi Tunzi, Miss Universe 2019

Zozi and Cheslie at the Miss USA 2020 pageant, which occurred during the COVID-19 pandemic

Cheslie cohosting the Miss Teen USA 2020 pageant

April and Cheslie visiting Fort Mill High School during
her Miss USA homecoming week celebration

Photo courtesy of Extra

Cheslie crowning Lizzo
during an *Extra* interview

David and April with their close
friends Lynne Girts and Dan Wilson

TOP: April and her two best friends, Cheslie and Lynne Girts

BOTTOM: Cheslie and April on New Year's Eve in New York, 2020

April during her training for the New York City Marathon

April running the 2021 NYC Marathon. Cheslie and Lynne were in the crowd.

April and Cheslie
on the beach in
the Turks and
Caicos Islands,
October 2021

Cheslie and
Asa in NYC,
summer 2021

TOP: David and Cheslie hanging out in New York City

BOTTOM: Cheslie and Page at a Billie Eilish concert in NYC, 2021

TOP: The older four children at the Billie Eilish concert in NYC (L to R: Page, Asa, Chandler, Cheslie)

BOTTOM: The four older children each had a bracelet permanently soldered on their wrists, to show their never-ending love for each other. Cheslie was laid to rest with her bracelet intact.

TOP: The older four children posing at our house.
Cheslie, Asa, Chandler are in the back, and Page is in front.

BOTTOM: Christmas 2021 (Back row: Chandler, Jet, Brooklyn;
Front row: Asa, Cheslie, Page, Raegan)

TOP: Cheslie and Paula Shugart after the 70th Miss Universe Pageant, held in Eilat, Israel, 2021

BOTTOM: The older four and their dad (L to R: Asa, Page, Rodney, Chandler, Cheslie)

TOP: The entire family at Chandler's college graduation from Coastal Carolina University, December 2018 (Back row: April, Asa, Chandler, David, Cheslie, Rodney; Front row: Page, Raegan, Brooklyn, Jet)

BOTTOM: The family at the 50 Most Influential Women gala in 2016, where April was recognized as one of the fifty (L to R: Chandler, Asa, Joyce Reece-Thomas [Cheslie's grandmother], Page, April, David, Cheslie, Tessa Simpkins [Cheslie's grandmother], Gary Simpkins [Cheslie's grandfather])

TOP: The family at a USC gala where a scholarship was established to honor
Cheslie (L to R: Chandler, Gary, Tessa, David, April, Joyce, Asa, Page, Rodney)

BOTTOM: April speaking at the 71st Miss Universe Pageant in New
Orleans, Louisiana, discussing the importance of mental health

Cheslie Kryst, the model

PART TWO

April's Story

Chapter 14

UNTIL WE HAD NOTHING LEFT

Sunday, January 30, 2022

Damn! I was running late because I'd forgotten to set my alarm. My exercise class started at seven, and there was no way I'd get there in time. Should I even bother? *Yeah, it'll be worth it.* That's what I told myself. *You just gotta keep pushing to get there, and next time, remember to set the alarm.*

Scripts kept playing in my head, trying to motivate me to get going. I sped all the way to class and arrived just in the nick of time, at 7:00 a.m. I'm always such a rule follower and almost never speed, and the guilt mixed with adrenaline had me fired up and ready to throw some weights around. I did my usual video recordings of me exercising on the gym floor, so I could watch my form later and maybe even post it on social media. It had been a great class!

I couldn't wait to get to my car to call Cheslie. She didn't work out on Sundays, so I knew she'd have time to chat.

As I headed home, I stopped at the first traffic light and pulled out my phone. She had already texted me—probably to say that she had an early assignment with *Extra*, and we'd talk later. I drove through a couple more intersections and then turned off the main road. I opened her text, thinking it would be short and that I could read it at a glance.

The first paragraph was indeed short:

First, I'm sorry. By the time you get this, I won't be alive anymore, and it makes me even more sad to write this because I know it will hurt you the most.

My brain couldn't register the words on the screen. I read them again and screamed from a place in my soul that I didn't know existed. My hands started shaking, and I couldn't catch my breath. I immediately called her number, but she didn't answer. Then I called David, my husband, and yelled, "Call the police! It's Cheslie!"

By then I was home, and I ran into the house screaming, "Call the police! She sent me a text! She said she's not alive anymore!" I tried to read the rest of her text message, but I couldn't. My legs kept giving out. My two sons came running downstairs because of all the screaming. They looked at me in both fear and confusion.

This can't be real. I need all of this to not be real, was all I could think.

David began reaching out to the family to ask if anyone had heard from Cheslie. Then he called the police. He has a way of being levelheaded and controlled in the midst of a crisis.

He got the New York City police on the phone. We told them what we knew at the time and begged them to send someone to check on her.

It was now 8:30 a.m. Ninety minutes had passed since she'd sent the text. I knew the chances of her being alive were slim, but I held on to hope.

We'll get through this, and I'll be there for her again. We're going to get through this. I'm coming, Cheslie—just hang on.

The police told us that medics were on-site, which was the sliver of hope I needed.

I ran to my computer and booked our flights to New York. We needed to be there. I needed to be there when she came to. My brain was at war with my heart, the former knowing she was gone and the latter clinging to the hope that she wasn't.

We called the police again and again, and every time they told us they didn't have any updates, and medics were on-site.

My two youngest boys, through eyes filled with worry and sadness, tried to comfort me while I crawled on the floor and balled up into the fetal position, wailing. Then I'd crawl around on the floor some more, weak from the trauma of what was happening and scared because I couldn't breathe. I tried to stand up but kept falling to the floor, crying and pleading with God. *Please! Please!*

David continued contacting our family, to tell them we hadn't heard anything from the police. We were all waiting—waiting for the police to tell us she'd been rushed to the hospital, or she was in stable condition, or something. Anything.

By late morning, David and I had raced to the airport and boarded the plane. My brain was in overdrive, thinking through a game plan after our arrival in NYC. Who I'd need to call, whether Cheslie would be conscious enough to talk to us, if she would need me to get anything from her apartment, and the list went on. David and I repeatedly discussed every detail that came to mind.

We kept nervously looking at our phones, waiting for an update from the NYPD. Waiting for them to tell us what hospital she'd been admitted to or what was going on. Surely, she had survived because it had been hours, and the police had never said she was gone.

At some point I realized the flight attendant was going through her preflight instructions and telling the passengers to put their phones on airplane mode.

I can't turn my phone off. I need to know where she is.

As the plane was taxiing on the runway, my phone rang. I answered, and it was the detective.

"I'm sorry to tell you, your daughter's no longer with us," he said.

I went numb. David began to sob.

I don't remember the plane landing or getting into the Uber to ride to the hotel. Hell, I don't even remember making hotel reservations. Our phones had been off during the flight, and when we landed and turned them on, they blew up. Text messages were rapidly coming in, and I didn't know what to do. I couldn't talk to anyone, so David became the contact person. I just needed everything to stop. *Just stop! Give me a second to breathe!*

The police never told me how she died, so I was confused. How was it that people knew she was gone?

Then the medical examiner called. I handed my phone to David and tried to zone out. I heard him say something about her falling.

She jumped.

I had this sickening flashback from when I'd visited Cheslie last year. We were in Hudson Yards, and she showed me this incredible structure that was a labyrinth of stairs. I remembered the sadness on her face when she told me they'd closed the structure to the public because of the number of people who'd jumped to their death from it.

The sound of traffic jolted me back to the present.

There I was again, unable to breathe. I kept instructing myself to inhale and exhale, inhale and exhale. I could feel a lump forming in my throat and tears welling up in my eyes. I wanted to be home in my bed. I wanted the clock to rewind. I wanted to be on the phone with my baby girl, FaceTiming each other, wearing our bonnets and talking about our day.

I walked into the hotel room and collapsed on the floor. My very soul wept. My lungs burned from crying so hard. I would just weep, expelling all the air in my lungs. And then, like a diver racing to break through the water's surface, I'd throw my head back, sucking in all the air I could, and weep all over again.

David and I cried until we had nothing left. And then it was time to call for help.

I phoned my best friend, Lynne. I was crying when she answered the phone. She tried to fill in the blanks of my scattered speech. She asked me where I was and said she would come and get me. I kept trying to tell her that my baby was gone, but the words wouldn't come out of my mouth. It seemed my heart knew that if I said it out loud, it would be true, and it couldn't be true. I handed David the phone, and he told her what had happened.

My mind flashed back to November, when I'd run the New York Marathon. After the race, Lynne, Cheslie, and I were eating pizza in our hotel room. My body was so tired from running that it was hard to stay awake. I kept trying to keep my eyes open and drink in the moment. I felt at peace, there with my two best friends. But now, Cheslie was gone, and we'd never have moments like that again.

Why was I having these stupid flashbacks? Was this my life passing before my eyes?

If this is it, I'm fine if you're about to call me home, God. Please just take me now.

We had people we needed to call. I didn't want them to hear it over the news. One of the calls was to Cheslie's friend and publicist, LaToya. I don't know how the media outlets got our phone numbers, but they were calling, texting, emailing, and sending DMs to every social media account I had. We needed her to protect us while we tried to figure out what to do. Amid missing her dear friend and client, LaToya erected a near impenetrable shield around us and our family, at a time when we were at our most vulnerable.

David finished the calls with our best friends and said, "Dan, Lynne, and Kay will be here tonight." They were coming to take care of us.

Monday, January 31, 2022

Neither David nor I had slept. We'd cried all night long. Like infants, we'd cry ourselves into exhaustion, doze off, wake up, and repeat. Finally, David said we should get moving, even though we didn't know what to do or where to go. There's no guidebook on what to do if your child suddenly dies in another state. David buzzed Dan to say we should get some fresh air and coffee and figure out our next step.

All I wanted to do was climb under the covers and wait for all of this to be over. I wanted to call my baby girl and talk with her like I did every single morning. I wanted to hear her voice and see her smile. I needed that in this moment. But I knew David was right—we needed to get moving. We got dressed and headed to the hotel lobby to meet everyone. I glanced at the television in the lobby, feeling anxious and afraid that I'd see a story about her on the news or that her face would appear on the screen.

While we stood there in the lobby, the trauma propelled my brain into protection mode. The mundane mental checklists that usually play like a recording in my head right before I drift off to sleep had spontaneously turned on.

I need to cancel the carpet installation, I thought.

A few weeks ago, David and I bought new carpet for our house, and it was scheduled for installation on February 2. I'd spent weeks preparing the house. We'd had to relocate all of the furniture on the second floor and in our bedroom. My house was in complete chaos because nothing was in its place.

I turned to David and said, "I need to cancel the carpet install." Then I searched for the number in my phone and called the company. *What should I say?* I wondered. *Do I say I need to reschedule because my daughter died, and I'm not at the house? Or do I say nothing and grit my teeth through the fake hospitality and bubbly voice of the person on the other end of the phone?* I chose the latter option. The rescheduler was now on the phone. "Good morning. How can I help you?" All I could think was, *Stop sounding so cheerful, dammit! My daughter just died. Show some f-ing respect.* That's what I wanted to say, but instead, I calmly answered her questions and pushed the install out thirty days.

I don't remember the walk to Starbucks. I felt nauseous being in New York without Cheslie. Every step was a reminder that she was gone. For the first time in over thirty years, I had no clue where my baby was. How could I be her mom and not know exactly where she was?

We stood in Starbucks, waiting for our coffees. I couldn't hear what anyone was saying. Their mouths were moving, but their voices sounded distant.

"April, are you ready to go?" someone said. It took me a minute to recognize the voice; it was Lynne.

"Yes, I'm ready," I said.

We started back to the hotel, and there was that nagging question again: *Where is my baby?!* My knees started to buckle, and I couldn't take another step on the sidewalk. As I sobbed, I felt everyone huddle around me. It was all I could do not to scream from the pain in my heart.

My brain switched to survival mode again. *Inhale, exhale. Inhale, exhale. Breathe...*

Somehow, we all made it back to the hotel. Kay took me to my room, and Lynne lagged behind so she could tell Dan and David that she and Kay were taking me home. I felt awful leaving David there to deal with everything. I wanted to be there for him, and I needed him to be home with me. But I couldn't stay, and he couldn't leave. As we said goodbye, he promised that he'd bring my baby home, and I knew his word was solid as a rock. That's what I needed—to have my baby home.

In the airport, I had a series of out-of-body experiences. My brain was fully aware of what had happened, what was happening, but my heart couldn't accept the truth and instead stayed wrapped in a protective cocoon. Every now and then, my heart would feel the pain of the reality that she was gone, then quickly retreat into the safety of the cocoon. I could hear Lynne and Kay talking with me about something, but my brain wasn't processing anything. It was standing guard, protecting my heart by making sure that triggering words and thoughts were kept at bay.

We pulled up to my daughter Page's apartment, and I went upstairs. I don't know who opened the door or how many steps I took before collapsing into my son's arms and weeping. I couldn't squeeze my children hard enough. As they cried with me, I could feel their pain, their sadness. I wanted to comfort them and help them, tell them everything would be okay, but I couldn't. It wasn't going to be okay. I felt completely helpless. My children needed their mom, and there I was, reduced to the most primitive action of trying to remember how to breathe.

Inhale. Exhale.

Inhale. Exhale.

If I stopped telling my body how to breathe, I would die.

I couldn't hold my body up anymore. My son was holding all of my weight.

I lost the fear of death in that moment. I stopped caring whether I lived or died.

My brain raced through the past forty-eight hours like I was watching a movie on rewind.

I composed myself enough to sit with the family that had gathered at Page's apartment. Sitting there in a room heavy with pain, I read Cheslie's text message:

First, I'm sorry. By the time you get this I won't be alive anymore and it makes me even more sad to write this because I know it will hurt you the most.

I love you mom and you are my best friend and the person I've lived for for years. I wish I could stay with you but I cannot bear the crushing weight of persistent sadness, hopelessness, and loneliness any longer. I've never told you these feelings because I've never wanted you to worry and because I hoped they would eventually change but I know they never will. They follow me through every accomplishment, success, family gathering, friendly dinner, and they are loudest during my failures, setbacks, and heartbreak. I've cried so hard my face has swollen and my teeth ache. I cry almost every day now like I'm in mourning. I've wished for death for years and I know you would want to know and want to help but I haven't wanted to share this weight with anyone.

Regardless of that, thank you, sincerely, for being there for me in some of my loneliest moments without me even telling you I needed you. My birthday, New Year's Eve when we watched the ball drop. Israel. You have kept me alive and ready to face another day because you answer every phone call, you are there for me at the drop of a hat, you listen to me and care when I tell you what goes on in my life, and you've always made me feel like you love me. I love you more than any person I've ever known. You've done nothing wrong and you've done everything right.

I no longer feel like I have any purpose in life. I don't know if I ever really did. I don't know what tomorrow or next month or a year from now holds but I don't believe it will provide me any advancement or happiness. It feels like God has forgotten me or is tormenting me or trying to teach me a lesson I'll never understand. I've pushed away most of my friends. And I can't fix any of it no matter how hard I've tried. So, I will leave and rejoin God in heaven and hope to find peace there. I don't want to leave but I genuinely feel like I have to if I want to escape my loneliness that feels like it has no end. I've fought against depression for a long time but it's won this time around.

There aren't enough words in the world to describe my love and appreciation for you. You are the perfect mom and I will love you forever, even in death.

Feel free to share this message. People should know that you're the best mom in the world and that you were the best mom to me that I ever could have hoped for.

Cheslie*

Asa drove me and my other sons home from Page's place. I tried to sleep, but all I could think was, *My baby has now been in heaven for two days. I hope it's as beautiful and peaceful as we imagine it to be. I hope she feels the most incredible sense of peace. I hope she's the happiest and most content she's ever been.*

While I wished her all good things, I missed her. Desperately.

• • •

I'd never felt this much pain in my entire life. The first trauma response I had was the complete loss of my appetite, and the inability to taste food. My five foot five, 140-pound frame of muscle and grit was dwindling. Every morning I woke up crying. I just couldn't believe that Cheslie was gone. We always started our day with a phone call or FaceTime. She'd be prepping for her day, and I'd be fixing my breakfast, doing my makeup, or any of the other morning routines I'd adopted. But now, like someone trying to walk across a cluttered room in the dark, I couldn't find my way back to my routine.

And nothing about my house was the same. All of the furniture was out of place, and I didn't know whether to move it back, leave it as is and keep apologizing for the chaos, or hide in my

---

* Cheslie's full text message has not been included. The omitted parts include her final wishes, electronic device logins and passwords, and a personal message of love to her family.

closet to escape my life that had been completely upended and rendered unrecognizable.

My closest family came back to the house with me, and we sealed ourselves in this fortress, only allowing our closest friends and family to penetrate the perimeter. We gave ourselves permission to grieve in our own way. We comforted one another, listened to each other, and consulted as a family with a psychologist, a grief counselor, and our pastor, who was helping us plan Cheslie's funeral.

My loss of appetite was taking its toll. In less than a week I was down ten pounds and counting. I didn't have anything to wear to the funeral because my clothes no longer fit. David, who had returned from NYC, took me shopping. I walked through store after store in a daze. Shopping had always been a fun event for me. I couldn't remember a time when I'd gone shopping that I hadn't FaceTimed Cheslie for fashion tips or sent her pictures from the dressing room to get her opinion. And now I was on my own, trying to do something that she and I had always done together.

In one of the department stores, I had my first of many panic attacks. I sat on the floor, trying to catch my breath. I felt like I'd lost control of my body. Maybe this was it—maybe this was what dying felt like.

Poor David, who worried about me nonstop, called our doctor. He was so scared, and I felt terrible for putting him through this. I eventually got myself under control, and he took me home.

At Cheslie's funeral, I kept thinking, *I have to survive this because my family shouldn't have to bury me this soon after losing Cheslie.* That was the one thin thread that held me together that day.

My grief and sadness increased, while my weight continued to decrease. I was nearing 120 pounds. My body began to react to the rapid weight loss. One day I was brushing my teeth and saw a small lump on my throat. Then I found another lump. I couldn't tell David. The worry would break him.

I found a third lump in a different location, and now it was time to call my physician. Discovering the lumps jolted me into survival mode. I wasn't ready to go. If I died, who would tell the world all the incredible things I knew about my baby girl? Who would protect her, even in death? That was my job.

I decided that whatever was going on, I would fight it.

The doctor took my blood pressure and looked alarmed when he saw how low it was. He sent me for blood work, and my white blood cell count was low. I was in trouble.

Back at home, as I continued to plan a celebration of life ceremony for my daughter, I was now also checking my blood pressure three times a day and praying that my frail body wouldn't give out on me. Not yet, at least.

I began to focus my energy on recalling all the amazing things about Cheslie. The more I talked about her, and the more people shared their own fond memories of her, the better I felt. It was as if my heart could rest from missing her and instead bask in remembering her.

I continued to share some of my memories of her on social media. It felt therapeutic. It reminded me that she'd had joy in her life. She'd had laughter and friends, experiences and memories. In those moments, I knew she was still with me. I could feel her presence even though I couldn't see her.

In spite of these brighter spots, my physical health continued to decline right along with my mental health. My depression kept getting worse, and I eventually reached the place where I needed to accept that this might not go well for me. I'd heard of people dying from a broken heart and thought maybe that's what I was experiencing.

My weight continued to decrease, the lumps hadn't gone away, and my blood pressure remained unstable. But I had to keep going. My husband needed me, my children needed me, and Cheslie needed me. She needed me to tell her story and save lives.

So I decided to do exactly that, and it began to make me feel empowered. I decided to become an advocate for mental health and wellness. I committed to being a voice for those battling mental illness and its challenges. In the midst of unbearable pain, loss, sadness, and grief, I found a new purpose for my life. I was going to fight for my health so that I could help others.

Chapter 15

LAST WISHES

In early 2021, Cheslie called me to share some news.

"Mom, I've been writing an article for *Allure* magazine, and I want you to read it."

"Sure, I'll read it. What's it about?"

"It's about turning thirty."

I read the draft and then called her to talk about it. I liked her transparency and how she was being real with her feelings and frustrations. I agreed with her that women often are discarded after a certain age. We discussed that for a bit and laughed while I cited the transition from being young to being considered "past my prime." I told her how much I loved the way she ended the article with a "take on the world" attitude. That was so her—a fighter ready to take on the next challenge.

In the original article draft, Cheslie had included the reason she once had an eight-day hospital stint: a suicide attempt. We had a frank and honest conversation about her sharing that story publicly. She explained why she was okay doing so, but she also knew she was trolled heavily online and didn't want that revelation weaponized against her. Ultimately, she did mention the hospitalization but didn't share the exact reason for it.

• • •

Six years earlier, I was packing up my desk in my home office when I saw Cheslie's name appear on my phone. I smiled and answered.

"Hello!"

"Hello, Miss April," a stranger's voice greeted me instead of my daughter's. I bolted upright from my chair.

"Where's Cheslie?" My mother's instinct told me something was wrong.

"Cheslie is here," the voice answered. "We're at the hospital. She didn't want me to call you, but I insisted."

My heart was beating so loudly I could hear it thumping in my ears.

"What happened?" I asked while I rushed to throw some clothes in a suitcase and hit the road. I needed to get to my baby girl, *now.*

"I'll let her tell you."

As fast as I could safely get there, I arrived at the hospital to talk with Cheslie in person. I needed to see her. I needed to lay eyes on my baby girl. But she didn't want me there, she didn't want me to worry, and she didn't want to have to explain. She didn't want to feel ashamed or embarrassed, or like she'd let me down.

Until that moment, I'd always thought Cheslie and I had a great relationship and could tell each other anything. We laughed and joked and talked about so many things. Everything, it seemed, except the truth about her mental health. Whenever I asked, she was always "okay." Except right now, she definitely was not okay.

I didn't know what her true condition was, but I didn't want to upset her. So I asked her one question: "What happened?"

She told me she'd had a bad headache and had taken some over-the-counter pain medication and lost count of how many. I knew she was omitting *a lot* of the story. She clearly wasn't ready to tell me the whole truth, and I refused to press her.

Her big sister, Page, joined us at the hospital. In our family, Page is affectionately called "the second mom." She has a love and authority with her siblings that earned her that moniker. Page's conversation with Cheslie was vastly different from mine, a little more confrontational. I guess that's what made our family dynamic unique—we balanced each other. As a sister and "second mom," Page could speak to her siblings with a bluntness that resonated with them and a love that embraced them. Her siblings knew that she would call them to the carpet on their stuff, but her five-foot-two frame would also not hesitate to take on anybody who dared to hurt her siblings.

When I spoke with the attending physician, I learned that Cheslie was under observation for liver damage and kidney injury, and her mental state.

I was in a panic. I prayed the prayer of desperation and bargaining that every parent prays in these moments: *If she pulls through this, we'll be inseparable, and I'll be there for her in every way she needs me, no matter the situation or circumstance. Please, God, give me a second chance with her, and I will cherish and make the most of every single day.*

In the days that followed, I consulted with physicians about Cheslie's physical health and with a psychologist about her mental health. They needed my permission to keep her in the hospital to further examine and monitor her mental state—against her will, if it came to that.

It was the hardest decision I ever had to make. I knew my daughter, and I knew that if there was one thing she'd never surrender, it was control of her own life. And now, I was faced with the dilemma of taking that control away from her.

I talked with David about how scared I was to let Cheslie be released, especially since she hadn't told me the whole truth about what had happened. Yet I was also afraid that if I gave permission for someone else to take control of her life, she might never trust me again or forgive me. In that moment, I didn't know what was right and what was wrong.

In the end, I gave them permission and conceded to deal with her wrath.

For years, I carried the guilt of that decision. Eventually, Cheslie and I talked through what had happened, and she told me how she was going to make some changes in her life, supporting her own mental health more moving forward, and explained what she needed from me—specifically, how I could support her. I believed that she secretly resented me for making the choice I did that day. If her resentment was the price I paid for that gut-wrenching decision, then so be it.

When I read the original *Allure* article draft, we talked about the situation again. She said, "Mom, I understand why you made that choice."

True to my word and promise to God, Cheslie and I became best friends and were inseparable from that point on. We stayed connected, in communication, and in each other's lives, even on her final day.

When I read her last message to me and her words "you've done nothing wrong and you've done everything right," I knew she was telling me that the choice I'd made in the hospital all those years ago was the correct one, and she didn't hold it against me or resent me for it. That was the peace I needed to reconcile a pain and burden I'd carried for a long time.

• • •

I didn't know she'd left behind a note in her apartment. It was simple and short.

I want to leave everything to my mother.

I learned about the note the same way the world found out about it: from a newspaper article. I couldn't understand why the police didn't tell me. How did a news outlet have information about a note left in her apartment? I ran through the timeline the morning of her passing and realized that she'd passed away before I'd read her text, before our first call to the police. As a matter of fact, by the time we contacted the police the morning of her passing, my daughter was already deceased. The police knew this yet had refused to tell us. Instead, for three agonizing hours they told us medics were on-site, when, in reality, my baby was already with the medical examiner and the police were sharing information with a newspaper, not her family.

I worked hard to move forward from the cruelty of the police withholding information and instead focus on the message my baby girl had sent me before she passed. Every sentence was written to help me understand, to help me grieve, to help me realize that her decision was not spontaneous. She was clear that she'd been battling persistent depression for years. That for years, she'd wished for death.

I cried hard when I finally read the words in her last text message, because I realized in that moment, my daughter was a fighter and yet she was gone. Every day she'd fought persistent depression, until she couldn't fight anymore. Despite the many ways depression tried to rob her of joy, with near-constant headaches, loneliness, hopelessness, sadness, and a feeling of unworthiness, she still found a way to smile, love, and give. Every day I'd had with her was a true gift from God. Every day she was here was a victory. Every person in her life—her family, her friends, her mentors, her supporters, her fans—as well as her faith, had helped her find a reason to fight for her life another day. I'm grateful for everyone who helped sustain her, prayed for her, called her, sent her a text, laughed with her, cried with her, broke bread with her, supported her. Thank you.

In her message, Cheslie shared her final wishes with me. I read them over and over and promised her I'd fulfill every one of them, no matter what it took.

• • •

In October 2021, Cheslie invited me to join Nia Franklin and her in Turks and Caicos. I said yes before she even finished asking. This wasn't going to be a regular vacation—it was a working vacation. Cheslie and Nia would be working on writing projects, and I would be tackling a project I'd been putting off.

I had an incredible time with two amazing women in one of the most beautiful places on earth. We rode bikes, played in the water, walked along the beach, dined together, and laughed a lot. Cheslie and I shared a bedroom that had two twin beds. We'd lie in our beds laughing and chatting and showing each other memes. We giggled like teenagers and laughed until we cried. We truly were each other's best friend.

Two months later, in December 2021, Cheslie and I took a trip to Israel.

She was going to be a judge and backstage cohost for the Miss Universe pageant, and I was her plus-one/assistant/confidant/photographer/etc. We had an incredible time together. She had a lot going on, but even with her intense schedule, we still found time to eat breakfast together in her room and sit on the sofa in her suite and talk and laugh until tears rolled down our faces. I thank God for that trip and all the memories we created.

That same month, she was thrilled to share with me that she was almost finished with her manuscript. I was excited for her. I hadn't read it, but based on her excitement, I knew it was something she was extremely proud of. And that brought me joy. I just knew that 2022 was going to be her year.

In January 2022, I read my daughter's final writing ever, a text message telling me, among other things, her last wishes. The second wish was this:

My book be published with recommended edits from my publisher.

I read every word Cheslie wrote in the manuscript. While her intention had been to write a book about a distinct period in her life—balancing her work as Miss USA, an attorney, and an *Extra* correspondent—she also gave a behind-the-scenes look into the mind, thoughts, feelings, and emotions of a woman battling and managing depression.

After I read the manuscript, I thought, *This is the only book my baby will ever write, and her words, her honesty in sharing her emotional and mental state, balanced with her vulnerability, are going to save lives. People will read this and relate to her.*

Chapter 16

A SUPPORTER, NOT A SAVIOR

After Cheslie's first suicide attempt, I tried to be a savior. I strived to carry her pain, so it wouldn't be as heavy for her. I was scared all the time. Scared of losing her or letting her down. This level of fear was maddening and paralyzing. I worried about her around the clock. I analyzed everything she said and didn't say. Silence was not golden—it was cause for alarm.

Most days, my mind raced through what-if scenarios: *What if she needs me and I miss her call? What if she's struggling right now? What if she's on the verge of catastrophe? I should call her. That'll make me feel better.* Scripts like that constantly played in my head. It wasn't healthy for me or for Cheslie. She even told me how stifling I was being.

I realized then that what she needed was a supporter, not a savior. I had to learn how to sit with her when she wasn't okay and understand that my role was simply to be with her, not to "fix" her. I needed to release the fear that permeated every part of me and give her the space and freedom to live her life. I learned to take my cues from her, and I learned how to truly listen to her.

No matter how much you love your child, you can still lose them. And I was determined not to miss out on loving her because of my fear of losing her.

After I did lose Cheslie, I refused to get sucked into the vortex of blame and guilt. Blame needs a target. Blame is like a ball of raw emotion looking for someplace to land. A ball of anger, hurt, pain, confusion, desperation, shame, and fear all rolled into a lethal weapon waiting to be hurled at someone or something. I refused to make space in my life for blame. Period. I wouldn't blame her counselor, employer, friends, family, myself, or her. No, I was not going to play the blame game. Blame is too dangerously close to guilt, another emotion that can crush your soul.

Guilt is like planting a permanent rearview mirror in front of you and staring at nothing else but that mirror, causing you to miss out on experiencing the present and not allowing you to focus on the future. Guilt leaves you stuck in self-blame, believing that you have the power to change a past that has already been written.

I knew in my heart of hearts that I had made the most of every moment with Cheslie. I answered every call, I held her when she cried from heartbreak, I raged with her when she felt betrayed—I was there for her in every way I could be. Allowing guilt into my grief journey would only serve to rob me of basking in every sweet moment we'd shared. I refused to let that happen. I begged God for more time with her after her first suicide attempt, and that's exactly what he gave me—more time, and for that I'm forever grateful.

Refusing to give into blame and guilt left me with intense grief and crippling sadness, and I had to learn to live with that. Cheslie didn't "do this to me" or anyone else. She felt unimaginable pain and needed that pain to stop. That is the struggle of many people battling persistent depression.

One tool I use to help myself in moments of grief and sadness is to refrain from starting sentences with certain phrases, like "I wish," or asking questions like, "Why didn't she tell me?" "What did I miss?" or "Why did she do this?" Few things will cause blame and guilt to sweep you away into agony like starting sentences with those words or asking those questions.

Instead, I start my sentences with the words "I'm grateful for," and I finish that sentence with my most vivid memories of Cheslie. I declare my gratitude for the years we had together, the trips, her laugh, her smile, her sense of humor, the talks, the tears, and the depth of our love for each other. I'm grateful for Cheslie's love for us, her family, and the magical energy that entered the room with her. I'm grateful for her infectious laugh, which came from her soul and instantly made people laugh and smile. I'm grateful for our road trips spent singing along to Beyoncé, talking about life, or sitting in comfortable silence. I'm grateful to her for inviting me into her life and making me her best friend.

Words and thoughts of gratitude didn't stop the waves of grief and sadness from washing over me. They served as an anchor that prevented me from being washed out to the bottomless ocean of pain.

I have never known a pain as deep as losing my baby girl, Cheslie.

Some days the pain runs so deep that all I can do is scream. Many days I patiently wait until I am alone in my home, so I can step into the shower and let the healing power of the water wash over me while I scream, cry, weep, and wail. When I finally reach the point of exhaustion, I just sit in the shower and let the water comfort me. Other days I sit in my car, crank up the music, and scream until I'm hoarse. I don't know why that tends to make me feel better, but it does.

● ● ●

Before January 30, 2022, my life had a rhythm. I knew exactly who I was and where I was heading. My daily routine was rock solid. I worked out, checked Instagram for Cheslie's workout pic in her story, got the boys off to school, and then called my baby girl to chat about the day ahead. When Cheslie died, my life took a sharp right turn, and the path I was on evaporated. I found myself facing a forest with no discernable path, no clear direction, no tangible instructions.

There I was, looking at a catalog through tears, trying to pick out flowers for Cheslie's casket. How was this even possible, when one week ago she and I had been laughing on the phone, sending selfies, talking about life, and now my family and I were planning her funeral?

When I learned that Cheslie died, it felt like someone busted into my world and incinerated my life. All traces of the April I'd known for more than five decades were gone, and missing among the rubble was joy. For me, joy was the hardest state of being to find and reconnect with. Joy is so different from happiness and laughter. I can fake happiness with a smile, but joy? I can't fake that. Joy emits from the soul and fills you with peace. After losing Cheslie, I believed I'd never feel joy again. How could I, when my soul was in such despair?

Fighting deep depression became part of my everyday life. Gone were the days when I'd wake up, scroll through pics of my kids on my phone, head out for a run, and patiently wait to talk with my baby girl. That routine was replaced with me lying in bed and softly weeping, hoping not to wake David. I mourned the life I used to love, I mourned the future my baby girl would never have, and I mourned the gaping, unfillable hole in our family. I hated this new routine. I wanted my old life back. I wanted Cheslie back.

The hardest part of healing has been learning to just feel what I feel. Allowing myself to do this is new for me. I was married and had my first child by the time I was twenty-one years old. My entire adult life, I've been a mother and/or a wife. I'm conditioned to ignore my own needs and take care of my family. I vividly remember a couple of weeks after I gave birth to my fifth child, Brooklyn, my oldest son, Asa, who was fourteen at the time, was impatiently waiting for me to drive him forty-five minutes away to his soccer practice. Mom duty doesn't stop or slow down, not even after having another baby. The urge to "stay busy" has always been my coping mechanism. If my brain was in overdrive and I stayed physically active, there was no time to feel anything. And that felt safe. But I couldn't "busy" my way through depression, anxiety, or grief. I had to learn to feel it—the weight of it, the pain of it.

Now I've learned to stop and clear space to feel what I feel. I've learned ways to do my own self-assessment of my mental and physical health. I had to seek help for my panic attacks that left me unable to drive or be physically alone. I began having panic attacks when I stopped busying myself and just allowed myself to be in the moment and feel. I fought the urge to retreat back into the familiar practice of numbing myself by staying busy. I was determined to change, and change I did. When I laugh, it comes from a place of pure happiness. When I smile, it's genuine. When I'm hurt, down, sad, or lost, I cry. And on those rare occasions when my extreme grief collides with my severe depression and I start spiraling, I survive.

• • •

Cheslie was an incredible woman. Just when I thought I knew all there was to know about her, I'd learn something new. I loved those moments of discovery. I'd listen to her tell me a behind-the-scenes story about an old picture she'd found, or she'd tell me her goals in great detail. She never ceased to amaze me.

One Sunday afternoon in Charlotte, Cheslie and I crossed paths with Justin, who was on his way to my son's place. This was long after Cheslie and Justin had closed the door on their relationship and moved on with their lives. The three of us stood together, catching up and laughing. It was good to see them so relaxed while in each other's company, leaving all they'd gone through together in the past—where it belonged. Watching her simultaneously hold a boundary while engaging in meaningful conversation was a masterclass in unbothered.

And now, I'm blessed with even more opportunities to learn new things about her because my home is filled with everything she held dear. Looking through photos, skimming her journals, reading her notebooks, and watching her video diary on her phone has allowed me the joy of continuing to learn something new about my baby girl each day.

For years Cheslie had sent me care packages filled with clothes, makeup, and lots of goodies she'd received and decided not to keep. I loved it when she'd text me to say, "A package is on the way." When it arrived, I'd be as giddy as a kid on Christmas morning, ripping open a box to reveal a long-awaited gift. But January 2022 was different. A box from her showed up on my doorstep, without any advance notice. I looked at the items inside and felt perplexed. Something about them seemed random. Some of them weren't gifts—they were her things.

Two weeks later, Cheslie and I were immersed in a deep conversation about death and suicide. Someone famous had lost their child, and a dear friend had recently lost her son, and we talked about this. I shared with her how much my heart ached for those two moms, and she reminded me of my strength, our bond, and our love. I'm thankful we had that conversation. I learned a lot that day when I sat in silence and just listened— really listened. In hindsight, my baby girl said all she needed to say to me that day.

After Cheslie passed, I reflected on everything that had transpired that January. And once I received and explored all of her electronic devices, it was clear to me that her passing was not an emotion-fueled, spontaneous decision. She'd fought persistent depression for many years and had grown tired of fighting. She'd sent me that final text message to comfort me and to explain the depth of the pain she had carried.

This part of my life's journey has reshaped who I am and who I want to be. My life's purpose has changed, and I realize more clearly my life's mission: to continue to shine a bright light on mental health and wellness. My hope is if you are struggling with your own mental health, you find comfort in knowing that someone out there understands you and is boldly and publicly speaking out on your behalf.

Battling mental illness can be exhausting, isolating, and lonely. I know there are times when you want to give up. Don't. Your life is worth living. I see you and I hear you. You are not alone. Please find strength in knowing there's an army of us pulling for you. On those really difficult days, breathe, give yourself space and grace, and live to fight another day.

AFTERWORD

from the National Alliance on Mental Illness

I never met Cheslie, but I feel like I know her.

Not only because I've become very close to her mom, NAMI ambassador April Simpkins, but because I, too, lost a close family member to suicide who was of Cheslie's same demographic at about the same age. And I, too, know what it's like to look like everything is okay on the outside yet still be struggling deeply within.

One thing has always been true of Cheslie: she was radiant, inside and out. It was (and it still is) evident to all just how much light she carried and shone onto everyone around her, despite the darkness she quietly battled when no one was around. Cheslie was a changemaker and an advocate for so many, and she will always be deeply missed.

In reflecting on Cheslie, we are reminded that anyone can be affected by mental health challenges—no matter how successful or bright or beautiful or talented they may be, or how collected or confident or put-together they may seem. We are reminded of how convoluted the causes of mental illness, suicide, tragedy, and loss can ultimately be to ascertain. And we are reminded of just how much our young people are struggling today, in an increasingly complex world with an impossible amount of pressure.

Cheslie spoke openly about the pressures she faced to achieve and keep up appearances—as a *young* person, as a young *woman*, as a young *Black* woman, as a young Black woman in highly competitive and performance-based fields like modeling, pageantry, television, and law. She carried a great deal of wisdom. If we didn't listen before, it's imperative that we listen now.

We all have a role to play in building a better world, fighting stigma, and preventing more tragic outcomes in the future. It starts with us having the courage to be vulnerable, the courage to reach out for help, the courage to ask people how they are *really* doing, and the courage to truly listen.

In the United States, one in five people experience mental health challenges each year. This means that if you're having a hard time, you're not alone. And if you aren't struggling, it's highly likely that—whether you're aware of it or not—you know someone who is.

Over the next few pages, we've provided a list of mental health resources. We hope you'll hold these resources closely in case you ever need them, or in case you ever need to share them with someone else who does.

We also hope you'll heed our call to action of regularly checking in on those around you, no matter how "fine" they seem:

- **Check in on your strong friends.**
- **Check in on your smart friends.**
- **Check in on your cool friends, your funny friends, your productive friends.**
- **Check in on your colleagues, your family, your loved ones.**
- **Check in on yourself.**

We must get beyond surface-level pleasantries and social media–filtered presentations of people's lives. We must put a stop to the stereotypes about what someone who is depressed is supposed to look like. We can't keep judging a book by its cover; we have to start examining the table of contents and reading all of the chapters within:

- **Ask people how they are really doing.**
- **Make space for them to truly answer.**
- **Listen like a life depends on it—you never know when it does.**

And remember, no matter how much it may feel like it at any given moment, *you are never alone.*

There are so many of us out here who care about you.

There are so many of us who want to help you.

There are so many of us who are committed to standing by you until things get better.

Don't give up.

—Daniel H. Gillison Jr.
Chief Executive Officer, National Alliance
on Mental Illness (NAMI)

RESOURCES

Organizations
- National Alliance on Mental Illness (www.NAMI.org)
- Anxiety & Depression Association of America (www.adaa.org)
- Bring Change to Mind (www.BringChange2Mind.org)
- National Council on Wellbeing / Mental Health First Aid (www.TheNationalCouncil.org)
- National Institute of Mental Health (NIMH) (www.nimh.nih.gov)
- American Psychiatric Association (www.psychiarty.org)
- Suicide Survivor support groups (www.save.org)
- Mental Health America (mhanational.org)
- Mental Health Coalition (TheMentalHealthCoalition.org)
- National Association of State Mental Health Program Directors (www.NASMHPD.org)
- Suicide Anonymous (suicideanonymous.net)
- Black Psychiatrists of America (blackpsychiatrists.org)
- Blue Dove (Jewish Mental Health Organization) (TheBlueDoveFoundation.org)
- National Latino Behavioral Health Association (nlbha.org)

- Boris Henson Foundation (Black Mental Health Organization) (BorisHensonFoundation.org)
- Trans Lifeline (TransLifeline.org)
- The American Foundation for Suicide Prevention (AFSP) (afsp.org)

Books

- *You Are Not Alone: The NAMI Guide to Navigating Mental Health* by Ken Duckworth, MD
- *Maybe You Should Talk to Someone* by Lori Gottlieb
- *An Unquiet Mind: A Memoir of Moods and Madness* by Kay Redfield Jamison
- *The Imp of the Mind: Exploring the Silent Epidemic of Obsessive Bad Thoughts* by Lee Bauer
- *Facing Serious Mental Illness: A Guide for Patients and Their Families* by Oliver Freudenreich et al.
- *Understanding Mental Illness: A Comprehensive Guide to Mental Health Disorders for Family and Friends* by Carlin Barnes and Marketa Wills
- *Devastating Losses: How Parents Cope with the Death of a Child to Suicide or Drugs* by B. Fiegelman et al.
- *Healing the Hurt Spirit: Daily Affirmations for People Who Have Lost a Loved One to Suicide* by Catherine Greenleaf
- *Survivors of Suicide* by Rita Robinson and Phyllis Hart
- *Spark: The Revolutionary New Science of Exercise and the Brain* by John J. Ratey, MD
- *The Tao of Fully Feeling* by Pete Walker
- *Permission to Come Home: Reclaiming Mental Health as Asian Americans* by Jenny Wang
- *The Joy of the Disinherited: Essays on Trauma, Oppression, and Black Mental Health* by Kevin Dedner

- *The Queer and Transgender Resilience Workbook: Skills for Navigating Sexual Orientation and Gender Expression* by Anneliese Singh
- *You Need Help: A Step-by-Step Plan to Convince a Loved One to Get Counseling* by Mark Komrad and Rosalyn Carter
- *Black Man in a White Coat: A Doctor's Reflections on Race and Medicine* by Damon Tweedy
- *The Unapologetic Guide to Black Mental Health: Navigate an Unequal System, Learn Tools for Emotional Wellness, and Get the Help you Deserve* by Rheeda Walker, PhD
- *Healing: Our Path from Mental Illness to Mental Health* by Tom Insel
- *Family Guide to Mental Illness and the Law* by Linda Tashbook

Podcasts and Other Media

- *Depresh Mode* with John Moe (podcast)
- *Am I Doing this Right?* with Corinne Foxx and Natalie McMillan (podcast)
- *The Healing Trauma* with Monique Koven (podcast)
- *The Anxious Truth: A Panic, Anxiety and Mental Health Podcast* with Drew Linsalata
- *The Mental Illness Happy Hour* with Paul Gilmartin (podcast)
- *The Trauma Therapist* with Guy McPherson (podcast)
- *Therapy for Black Girls* with Joy Harden Bradford (podcast)
- *Welcome to My Breakdown* with Miyam Bialik (podcast)
- *Real Feels* with Brad Gage (podcast)

- *The Me You Cannot See*, produced by Oprah Winfrey and Prince Harry (documentary available on Apple TV)
- *Touched with Fire* directed by Paul Dalio (film)
- *NAMI Compartiendo Esperanza* (video series)

Other Resources

- National Suicide Prevention Lifeline (9-8-8)
- 741741 Crisis Text Line
- University of Michigan National Network of Depression Centers
- NAMI Blog, including recovery stories, tips, and professional perspectives

ACKNOWLEDGMENTS

Cheslie trusted me with her final wish of getting her book published. I had no idea what the journey would entail. I only knew that my baby girl had a dream, and I was going to do everything in my power to see to it that her dream came true. I'm at a bit of a loss here because I never had the chance to talk with her about all the people who played a role, big or small, in this project. I know there were many of you, and to you, I say thank you. Thank you for listening to her, and supporting and encouraging her while she was writing her manuscript.

David, I've struggled to find the words to describe how much I appreciate you and the depth of your support. We've been through so much together and here we are, still going strong. Every time you held down the fort and made space for me to hurt, grieve, cry, rage, and heal, it reminded me of how great of a husband you truly are. I appreciate all the times you listened to me talk about this project and encouraged me to keep going. I love you. Thank you, honey, from the bottom of my heart.

To Asa, Page, Chandler, Brooklyn, and Jet you will never know how many days loving you kept me alive. Cheslie is irreplaceable, and no family event will ever be the same without her. I know losing her has been beyond tough and extremely emotional for you. Please continue to take the time and space you need to manage your grief. She loved you guys so very much, and so do I.

My dear sweet Lynne, Dan, and Kay, I could say thank you a thousand times and it still wouldn't be enough. The way you rescued us in New York and took care of our family when we got back meant the world to us. We've had quite a journey over the past decade and a half. So many good times, memorable moments, celebrations, and heartaches. I love you. Thank you for being such incredible friends and for reminding me, on the darkest, most painful days of my life, that I'm not alone.

Tate, you were a wonderful boss and mentor to Cheslie. Your commitment to her success as an attorney and her continued legacy in the legal profession shows how much you and the team at Poyner Spruill cared for her not just as a colleague, but as a person and friend. I know she had many great memories from working with you and others there at the firm, and I speak for her and our family when I say you all have gone above and beyond to ensure that she will not be forgotten. Thank you.

Paula, thank you from the bottom of my heart for letting me travel as Cheslie's plus-one to so many unforgettable pageants. The time she and I shared in Eilat, Israel, was absolutely magical. You and the Miss Universe Organization were so good to Cheslie and so hospitable to me, and for that, I'm eternally grateful. Thank you for being my friend, my rock, my confidant, my lunch date, and my dinner date. Thank you for every moment you cared for Cheslie. I know you had a special place in her heart and that she loves you, and so do I. Esther, thank you for watching over Cheslie during her days as Miss USA. From the moment we met in Reno, I knew she was in good hands. You took care of her at a time of great transition in her life, and you made sure she was okay. I love you for that. Thank you.

Marie, thank you for giving Cheslie the career opportunity that she truly loved. I remember the day she called me to tell me about her interview. She was so excited, and I was happy and nervous for her. After she became part of the team and began interviewing, I saw a new side of her. I thoroughly enjoyed hearing about her day, the interesting people she was interviewing, and of course, her behind-the-scenes bloopers that always left us both laughing so hard we'd cry. Yvette, you are an incredible producer and friend. You were more than a coworker to her—you were family. Thank you for all you've done and continue to do for Cheslie. You've always had her back. Thank you for her birthday party, the long talks, the introductions, everything. You are such a wonderful, kind, and caring person. I'm so thankful to have you in my life. I love you. And to the rest of the team at *Extra*, I share my heartfelt gratitude for all you did and continue to do for my baby girl.

Nia, you are one of the most amazing and beautiful women I've ever had the pleasure of knowing. Thank you for being such a special part of Cheslie's life and embarking on this journey with her. I know if Cheslie were writing this it would be filled with undying gratitude, love, and appreciation for a friendship born out of the sisterhood of pageantry. You are as precious to me as a daughter, and I love you.

Amanda, even though we didn't meet until after my baby girl passed, I know it was Cheslie who brought us together, and our friendship was meant to be. You are such a ray of sunshine, and I clearly see why Cheslie and you worked well together on this project. You are an amazing editor, and I'm so grateful to God that you and I got to work together. Thank you for your words of encouragement, for sitting with me during my moments of deep grief and utter despair. Thank you for gently yet intentionally encouraging me to not give up on fulfilling Cheslie's wish. This was such a long road full of setbacks and a fair share of disappointments, but we persevered and got it done. Cheslie always said if it's God's plan, nothing can stop it or change it. This, I know, was part of God's plan. #MentalHealthAwareness #SavingLives

Matthew, when I first met you in Florida at the Miss Universe pageant, I knew you were sharp, professional, and great at what you do. Thank you for being Cheslie's agent and friend. Your help and guidance in bringing this project to life has been invaluable. You and Haley did a wonderful job of giving us space to grieve and process before embarking on moving this project forward. I appreciate every phone call we had and the many times you gave me words of support and encouragement in the midst of my grief and pain. Your commitment to helping and intervening on our behalf has meant everything. I know our paths will continue to cross because of our mutual pledge to protect and honor Cheslie's legacy. Thank you for everything—you're the best.

My dearest Dan, I don't even know where to start. From the first time we talked, I was ready to commit to the mission and work of NAMI. You are one of the most compassionate people I've ever met. Every time we talk, I feel enlightened and emboldened to keep pressing forward with my work as a mental health advocate. You are more than a friend—you are family. Thank you to Traci, the entire team at NAMI, and my local chapter NAMI Piedmont Tri-County for supporting me and reminding me that we are doing good and necessary work, breaking the stigma and shining a light on mental illness.

Thank you, Jonathan, and the team at Forefront Books for working with me and mentoring me through this project. Your support and effort contributed to pushing Cheslie's wish across the finish line. From editing to cover design, you helped bring this project to life. Thank you for believing in this project and the good it will do to save lives and remind people that they are not alone. Thank you also to Simon & Schuster for the work you put into seeing that this book is distributed and available to any and everyone.

Finally, to every person who loved Cheslie, touched her life, and made the commitment to carrying her legacy forward, from the bottom of my heart, THANK YOU.

ABOUT THE AUTHORS

Cheslie Kryst was a complex civil litigation attorney, licensed to practice law in both North and South Carolina. Passionate about criminal justice reform, she worked pro bono for clients serving excessive time for low-level drug offenses. Cheslie was crowned Miss USA in May 2019 and represented the United States at the 2019 Miss Universe Competition, placing in the top ten of ninety countries.

In October 2019, Cheslie was named a correspondent for the nationally broadcast entertainment news show *Extra*, where she regularly interviewed the world's biggest names, celebrities, and influencers.

April Simpkins is a mental health advocate, serving as an ambassador for the National Alliance on Mental Illness (NAMI) and a board member for NAMI Piedmont Tri-County, where she serves her local community. She has earned a Mental Health First Aid Certification and is also trained in Emotional CPR. As a C-suite executive, April is an in-demand public speaker who has addressed audiences internationally on the topics of leadership, culture, DEI, and mental health in the workplace. She has received numerous awards for her business acumen and community service.

April is the wife of David, the mother of six incredible children, and the grandmother of one beautiful granddaughter.